SPORTS MINISTRY THAT WINS

Smith J. & English G. (Eds.). (2001). Sports ministry that wins. Omaha, NE: Cros Training Publishing.

JIMMY SMITH, PH.D
EDITOR
GREG ENGLISH
CONTRIBUTING EDITOR

Sports Ministry that Wins

Gonzaga University
School of Education
Sport and Physical Education
502 E. Boone Ave
Spokane, WA 98258

ISBN 978-1-938254-63-5

Sports Ministry that Wins / Jimmy Smith
Published by Cross Training Publishing and
The Association of Church Sports and Recreation Ministries (CSRM), Overwhelming Victory Press
Omaha, Nebraska 68137
www.crosstrainingpublishing.com
www.csrm.org

Distributed in the United States and Canada by Cross Training Publishing

This book is manufactured in the United States of America.

Table of Contents

FOREWORD

by
Rev. Danny Downing
Associate Pastor, Sports & Fitness
Johnson Ferry Baptist Church, Marietta, Georgia
www.johnsonferry.org/youthsports
@dannydowning
Former CSRM Board Chair

Coach Steve Smith. You can say that name to anyone who went to high school with me and they will not only know who you are talking about, but also smile remembering him. He had a positive influence on so many of us. He treated us fairly and with respect. Bigger than that, it was clear that he cared. For me, he was the first coach who recognized the person I could become. He challenged me to grow not only as an athlete and leader, but also as a follower of Christ. He confirmed in me a calling into ministry. We all know a Steve Smith. I bet you can think of someone from your childhood who had a tremendous impact on you as well.

What do you love to do? What do we have in common? We want to make a difference! We long to have a positive impact on the people around us. As a coach, you want to influence your players. As a Sports Minister or Leader, you want to reach and disciple people for Christ. One of the greatest joys I have had in ministry is baptizing players that our league has introduced to Jesus Christ! Our church does a special children's baptism service and I get to say some encouraging words about each child as I introduce them and then what a privilege it is to baptize them. It is an awesome reminder for me that what we do in sports ministry is of the utmost importance. Sports Ministry can, and should be, the most effective tool your church uses to reach and engage your community.

We live in a sports-crazed culture and serve an amazing God. We have the honor of using the thing we love, sports, to tell those around us about God's love for them. It is our responsibility to be so effective in what we do that more and more churches will have no choice but to add sports ministry.

The fact that you have this book in your hand tells me you have a desire to win! *Sports Ministry that Wins* offers a practical blueprint for building and managing a sports ministry that is Gospel-Centered. Jimmy and Greg have done a masterful job giving us the building blocks for a successful sports ministry. They have combined the philosophical and the practical in a way that will help all of us be intentional in our sports ministry efforts. My hope and prayer is that this becomes a textbook for Introduction to Sports Management and Sports Ministry classes being taught around the country.

This book will be especially helpful to the sports minister beginning in ministry that did not have the opportunity to take sports ministry classes. Perhaps your school only offered secular, sports management classes—*Sports Ministry that Wins* will be a great resource in helping translate what you learned and apply it to church ministry. Maybe you were called into sports ministry after finishing your education. No worries! God will combine your faithfulness and passion for ministry with the concepts in this book to build a ministry pleasing to Him!
Does a veteran in ministry need to read this book? Absolutely! In our sports ministry at Johnson Ferry, I have the honor of training sports ministry associates. I also get to work with interns and introduce them to the idea of sports ministry in the local church. *Sports Ministry that Wins* is a book that will help me tremendously as I train associates and interns in sports ministry. It will be required reading!

One of the things that is so great about this book is the variety of contributing authors. Jimmy and Greg did an amazing job of enlisting authors from different size programs and churches who varied in their experience and position. You will hear from those in the trenches of sports ministry to some who have been there and give wise advice based on their experiences. Some authors are the only staff member and some have staff members who report to them. What a great opportunity you have to learn from all of them!

Do not just read this book and put it on a shelf. Keep it handy. Make notes in the margins, read the sidebars, and take the time to do the Learning-to-action exercises. From time to time, go back over the book as a reminder of doing what it takes to win!

DEDICATION

I dedicate this handbook to my family and friends that supported me throughout my career and continue to do so. Thank you. I also dedicate this handbook to the future sport managers and sport ministers to give them the strength to provide a social contribution in their communities. I would also like to thank Niagara University and Gonzaga University for their support in my sport ministry research. Finally, I thank the Good Lord for bringing "The Gregs" into my life. This handbook would not have been possible without them.

Jimmy Smith, Ph.D.

100% of the sales of this handbook go to benefit the sports ministry efforts of the Gonzaga University Sports Outreach Initiative and the Association of Church Sports and Recreation Ministries

PREFACE

Over the past few years I have conducted research (and continue to do so) related to managing sports ministry programs. Learning more about sports ministry and the faith communities they serve has resulted in my own understanding of how I can better serve the Lord. This is my hope for you in reading this handbook, that you find your own way to serve the Lord (even if it is not through sports ministry…but we certainly hope it is) or to strengthen your current service to the Lord through your sports ministry. During my research I have had the opportunity to speak with numerous sports ministers around the country to discuss how they manage their programs. These conversations led me down a path where I believe that the Lord gave me the strength to bring the ideas of this handbook to you.

During my discussions with sports ministers I noticed a theme… a strength…an expertise if you will. That each individual I spoke with had a specific passion that overwhelmed their successes and helped them through some challenges as a sports minister. I could hear these passions through the words they spoke and the tone in their voices about how they managed their programs. It was encouraging. I quickly realized an opportunity for the greater sports ministry community. Developing a handbook that would be an educational resource for current sport ministers and soon-to-be sports ministers. Personally, I was trained as a sports manager, being a collegiate baseball player and working in three different college athletic departments in several managerial capacities and now being a sport management professor at Gonzaga University in Spokane, Washington. With my past personal experience and my research of sport ministers I could see the connection between how a university and its athletic department are structured and how a church and its sports ministry program are structured. The hierarchies have similar qualities. These connections made sense to me. I wanted to couple my sport management expertise with the sports minister's expertise that each of these chapter authors have, to provide you with an opportunity to become better sports ministry managers. And present this knowledge differently than any other sports ministry book out there.

Each of these authors has vast experiences in this field. I wanted to work with each of these authors to advance the understanding of what it takes to be successful in the field of sports ministry as well as managing any challenges that sports ministers may face. Did we cover everything that needs to be covered in this book, not likely, but I believe that to grow the field of sports ministry we all have to continue to educate ourselves to become better at managing our sports ministries. I firmly believe that as we become better managers, we become more efficient and effective and our ministries are able to grow because of it. By doing so, we can then become more efficient and effective with our programs and the greater goodness of the Lord can flourish throughout.

What you can expect from this handbook

Learning-to-action

As you may have noticed, I have not called this publication a book, as I believe that often times a book is read, and put on a shelf to collect dust. I wanted to categorize this as a handbook, so that it can be used time and time again. This handbook was designed for you, the reader, to use it, write in it, refer back to it and maybe even generate discussion from it with your fellow sports ministry managers.

You will find that at the end of each chapter there are Learning-to-Action exercises. These exercises are to encourage you the reader to do one or all of the above. Being an educator and researcher I found that many of the best ways for students to absorb what they learn from education materials and from the classroom is to activate their learning within 48 hours from their first interaction with new knowledge. I felt that a learning-to-action activity would encourage you to reflect on each chapter to participating in a short activity related to the overall topic or key highlights of the chapter. Some activities may be simple and other may be more thought provoking, but all encourage you to think about what you just read. These exercises were designed for you to get the most out of this book…to get you involved in turning what you learned from that chapter to action.

Additional reading resources

I am an advocate of finding time in your personal and professional life to continue your education. I have gone through 10 years of higher education from an undergraduate degree, to a master's degree to completing my Ph.D. But yet I still continue to take classes as I am currently taking MBA classes. I do this to not only advance my knowledge in areas that I think I am deficient, but to hone my craft as a teacher by learning other teaching techniques from my peers.

I commend you for reading this handbook and advancing your own knowledge, but it does not stop there. Many of the chapters within this handbook use Additional Reading Resources to highlight topics made in the chapters. All of these resources were collected and listed in the back of this handbook. My advice to you, if you write or highlight a passage within this handbook and it crosses over a resource the chapter author used, I challenge you to find that resource in the back of this handbook and continue educating yourself on that topic by locating that additional reading resource at your local library. With the technology we have at the tip of our fingers these days, you may be able to find all of the additional reading resources quickly.

Sports ministry?...All of the above!

As you will see in this handbook, sports ministry takes many forms in many different areas across the country, from a basketball team, to a small church, even at your local YMCA. Often times the term sports ministry is amalgamated to take on a different term or phrase. Without taking away from the authors message, I chose to keep other sports ministry terms the way they are presented within the chapter, but essentially they all mean sports ministry. You will see the following: Recreation ministry; Sports and recreation ministry; Sports, recreation and fitness ministry, and sports outreach to name a few. I also know other sports ministers that simply use the sports they specialize in as their 'ministry' title: Basketball ministry; Volleyball ministry; Skate ministry. Regardless of the term used the message is clear in that sports ministers are using sports and physical activity as a means to speak the Good News of the Lord to their participants. It should be noted that the authors of each chapter are affiliated with a church in their community. There are many other forms of sports ministry around the world including the "para" sports ministry field, such as the YMCA, Athletes in Action, Fellowship of Christian Athletes, and many more. While not having a contributing chapter author from a para-ministry could be considered a limitation, it is not without strategic considerations, and the future of *Sports Ministry that Wins* publications.

The Bible

Many of the authors utilize scripture to highlight their broad message within their chapter. This handbook has several authors from different denominations. While myself and the other authors of this handbook encourage you to utilize the Bible throughout your personal walk with the Lord, managing your sports ministry, and even reflecting on the passages within this handbook, we also wanted to be consistent with the scripture used for this book, therefore all versus cited within this handbook are from the following Bible version:

Crossway Bibles. The ESV Study Bible. Wheaton, IL: Crossway Bibles, 2008.

Themes

There are several themes that ring throughout this handbook. Themes such as leadership, building relationships, and the topic of church mission and vision are just a few that are discussed multiple times. Whether your ministry is just beginning or it has been established for a number of years, these themes (among others in this handbook) are very important topics and should be treated as such in your ministry and we hope that you can build discussions with your ministry team members or your colleagues regarding these topics.

Sidebars

Sidebar notes throughout this handbook feature managerial concepts to add to your knowledge and understanding of the chapter topic.

One area of importance regarding this handbook is the ***sidebar*** notes you will find strategically placed in the margins throughout the chapters. I anticipate that you will be engrossed in many of these chapters you read, but I wanted you to be aware of certain managerial terms or phrases to add to your educational experience. Be on the lookout for sidebars, as they may also be beneficial to your learning and the learning-to-action section at the end of each chapter.

Chapter highlights

Each of the 10 chapters within this handbook have managerial components to them to enhance your understanding of becoming a better sports minister. Each chapter was broken up and placed into a theme based on three broad topics including (1) forming a foundational context for understanding the essence of a sports ministry. This is where sports ministers begin to understand how to initiate their sports ministry. (2) Leadership development is significant to your sports ministry to be able to find the right volunteers to assist you in building and delivering your program and Good News. (3) Managerial applications are necessary for continuing to build, grow, and then maintain this success for years to come.

Theme: Context for sports ministry

Chapter 1 - Forming the foundation of a sports & recreation ministry

Why should you start a sports ministry? How does someone start a sports ministry? Rich Green and Steve Quatro create a two-part chapter to shed light on answering these questions for those interested in starting a sports ministry, but do not know where to begin. Each author provides building blocks for a new sports ministry in addition to key fundamentals for a successful sports ministry program. Not only is this chapter great for those that want to start a sports ministry, but those that have an established sports ministry, this chapter can ground experienced sports ministers to 'get back to the basics,' to re-evaluate their ministry and possibly reboot their ministry.

Chapter 2 – Possibilities for sports ministry in a small church

According to the National Congregation Study (NCS) hosted by Duke University, there are approximately 300,000 churches in the United States, many of which are small churches. Joe BW Smith discusses how to overcome the challenges a small church may face when starting a sports ministry program. Smith suggests that you may not have to have a physical sports ministry in your church to have a sports ministry in your community.

Chapter 3 – Evangelism and sports ministry

That first conversation with one of your sports ministry participants can be tough. How do you start this conversation? Will they be turned off by what you say? Will they come back? Jake Medcalf discusses the importance of speaking about the Good News in his chapter. He stresses the importance of removing the evangelistic agenda, love those for who they are and speak the Good News, and as Jake explains, it may be a matter of life and death.

Theme – Leadership in sports ministry

Chapter 4 – Leadership and leadership development in sports ministry

Developing good leaders is the by-product of being a good leader. Chris Phillips uses his background in sports management and years of experience leading other sports ministers to focus his chapter on leadership and developing leaders.

Chapter 5 – Counteracting a lone ranger leadership mentality

Many of you may have the support to start a sports ministry program, but you may be the only person within your faith community that has been designated to manage and lead this program. Tinsley Jones is one of those individuals and has been doing it for years. I asked Tinsley to write this chapter because I know that many that read this handbook may need to begin their ministries on their own. And even if you are not on your own Tinsley offers her perspective of managing a sports ministry program addresses the likelihood that those that manage a ministry on their own may fall into a Loan Ranger leadership mentality. Even if you are not on your own, it is the ability to identify that sometimes, we may all fall into the Lone Ranger mentality in some way in our lives.

Chapter 6 – Leading Coaches: How to approach coach recruiting, training and retention?

Bob Schindler uses his 30 years of experience in working with hundreds of coaches to detail one of the toughest aspects being a sports

[1] Approximate Distribution of U.S. Protestant and Other Christian Churches by size based on NCS study (excluding Catholic/Orthodox)

minister, recruiting, training and retaining coaches. Bob offers the reader wonderful advice and several techniques keep coaches coming back year after year.

Theme – Management of sports ministry

Chapter 7 - Marketing for the local church sports ministry

Flyers and church bulletin announcements may be a thing of the past when marketing your sports ministry program. Greg English and I discuss several branding and marketing strategies that may help promote your sports ministry program and increase your participation rates for years to come.

Chapter 8 – Sports ministry management with limited space

It is often sports ministry programs are not established because space is limited. David Waddell draws on personal experience as an athlete as well as a sports minister to provide a great interpretation of how to overcome space limitations and still provide a great ministry through sports and recreation.

Chapter 9 – Conflict Management within Sports Ministry: "It's not if it happens, but when it happens..."

It will happen…an argument…a falling out…poor communication. It will happen. Greg English discusses his experiences with conflict and how to manage conflict related to your sports ministry. Not only does Greg provide insight into managing conflict in a faith community setting, but he also teams up with fellow sports minister Jenny Young to develop a case study activity to enhance conflict management preparation and resolution.

Chapter 10 – Measuring ministry effectiveness: Tracking and reporting ministry opportunities

As a sports minister, you will almost certainly find yourself having a discussion with your senior pastor (or other stakeholders) about the benefits of the sports ministry program. The dreadful question may arise, "Why should we keep this sports ministry program afloat." You may need hard evidence to show your senior pastor the impact of the sports ministry program. Dave Bundrick brings that hard evidence to life and shows how tracking and reporting ministry opportunities can concretely show how your sports ministry program is impacting the community.

Conclusion

In my research in speaking with numerous sports ministers about how they manage their programs I began to realize that many of these ministers showed an imbalance between their sports programs they delivered and the ministry they delivered. Often times it was their ministries that fell short of their expectations. I firmly believe that by reading this handbook, participating in the learning-to-action activities, taking advantage of additional reading resources, and building your network of sports ministers in your community and around the country, you can improve your efficiency, effectiveness and managerial capacity to provide and equally outstanding sports ministry program.

All the best to you…God Bless.

Jimmy Smith, Ph.D.
Gonzaga University
School of Education
Sport and Physical Education

CHAPTER ONE

FORMING THE FOUNDATION

of a Sports & Recreation Ministry

PART 1 & 2

We wanted to provide the sport minister an opportunity to understand the functions of starting a sports ministry.

Rich Green and Steve Quatro provide these unique perspectives in starting a sports ministry program. While Rich and Steve shed light on the basics of starting a sports ministry, there are two approaches that a sport minister could take to starting a program. Rich outlines an Administrative approach and Steve outlines a Relational approach in starting a sports ministry. A sport minister could start with one approach or the other, or even combine both administrative and relational. Either way, both Rich and Steve provide great starting points in your quest to build a ministry and become a winning sports ministry manager. Enjoy!

Jimmy Smith, Ph.D.
Greg English

PART 1 - ADMINISTRATION

Fostering a vibrant and impactful sports & recreation ministry in YOUR Church

Rich Green - Care & Support Pastor
Compass Christian Church
Colleyville, TX
@BoileRich
Former CSRM Board Chair

I guess the best place to start when writing a chapter related to getting a sports ministry program off the ground is to answer the question…The elephant in the room question…Why?

The WHY:

Over my 30 plus years of ministry, 9 years with the Fellowship of Christian Athletes and over 20 years of doing Sports and Recreation Ministry in the local church, I have seen what an effective and powerful ministry tool Church-Based Sports and Recreation Ministry can be. When contemplating why a Sports and Recreation Ministry is vibrant and impactful tool for the local church, I start with the benefits to the local church. So with that in mind here are just a few of the benefits to consider.

1. Sports ministry is by far one of the best and most impactful ways for the local church to engage with its community and literally the world. As we see on a daily basis, the dramatic influence sports have on the American culture (positively and negatively), but it is not just the 'good ole US of A' that sports influence when it comes to culture. Since the days of the penning of the scriptures, and even before, sports have influenced the human culture. As I write this chapter the Olympic Games are on in the background and I marvel at the breadth of the impact sports has on the entire world.

Building a sports ministry is about meeting people and building relationships (as one of the major themes to this handbook high-

Community & building relationships

lights). You want to have an opportunity to meet people where they are? They are at sporting events as participants, coaches, fans, and supporters in our communities. What Jesus did was to meet people where they were. He did not say, "Hey come see me!" He went to them, and spent his time with them. Jesus went to where the people were. In literally every community where our churches are located people are engaged in sports at multiple levels. Just as Christ did, the church needs to meet people where they are. Go out and meet people!

Jesus was not the only one who thought meeting people where they are was important. When you look at the writings of Paul, he was like-minded. He writes the following to the church at Corinth…

I have become all things to all men so that by all possible means I might save some. I do all this for the sake of the gospel that I may share in its blessings.
(1 Corinthians 9:22-23)

If you look at Paul's writings, in his letters to the churches, it is littered with sports analogies, because Paul knew the people he was writing to would relate to them. You want to make an impact on your community, you want to meet people where they are, sports and recreation ministry is one of the most effective ways to help you reach that goal. People love to talk about sports, why not sports ministry.

2. It is a practical, non-threatening, and effective way for reaching those who are far from Christ. People will not darken the doors of a church, they will play softball, flag football, take fitness and Camp Gladiator classes, not only for the thrill of the sport, but because they want to be part of community. It is in the community of sports that life lessons are both taught and caught…Physically, emotionally, and most importantly, spiritually.

Here is the point, the impact you can have on the lives of those participating with you in your sports & recreation ministry can be dramatic, and life changing. If through the participation one has in your ministry you can take them from one who does not even acknowledge the existence of God, to the point of acknowledgement that perhaps God is real, that is a WIN. That is the kind of practical impact, and life transformation a recreation ministry can bring to your church.

3. A sport and recreation ministry offers a plethora of opportunities to build up and disciple the believers in your church. Recreation ministry is a "yes - and" proposition for the local church. YES, it is an opportunity to engage the world and reach those who are far from Christ, AND it is a wonderful opportunity to help followers of Christ to grow in their faith and in their hearts to serve others.

Here is what happens to a follower of Christ when they participate in a sports and recreation ministry of your church: through the participation in team/class devotionals, they are not only experiencing practical ways to apply God's word, but they are given the opportunity to share their story and how God has impacted their life—for others to see and hear. Other ways are the influence followers of Christ in your ministry is the positive message being heard through music in a class or program participation (i.e., Fitness classes), spiritual conversations happen throughout the participant's experience in your ministry, and the opportunity to serve others is available at multiple levels in a sporting ministry environment.

So when we consider the "Why?" it is important to note that sports and recreation ministry gives us the opportunity to teach about life and the Lord! Sports and recreation ministry gives us the opportunity to reach those we may otherwise never reach, and to grow those who are seeking after Him in ways that are unique to any other ministries of the local church.

Need more you say, as to why sports and recreation ministry in the local church? ***Here's why...***

1. Social, economic, and cultural barriers can be broken down through the mutual interest of sports. It and music are the "universal languages."

2. It provides a non-threatening "holding tank" for those far from Christ to be in while God breaks through the spiritual barrier. "Common Ground" opportunities.

3. Provides an environment for Christians to be "salt" and "light" in real-life situations. (Adults & Kids).

4. It creates an attractive area for believers / volunteers to be trained for further ministry. At many levels it is a great entry-level volunteer opportunity.

5. It provides legitimate recreation / fellowship opportunities for the body of Christ.

6. It is one of the best ways to intentionally engage with your community.

7. It supports and compliments other ministries of the church.

This is just a snippet of why I believe so passionately that sports and recreation ministry in the local church is not only a viable ministry for the local church, but one of the most effective opportunities our churches have to change the world! So great, without question sports and recreation ministry is ministry we should definitely consider being a part of our church, but how do we build it?

A **strategic plan** focuses on the entire sports ministry program's overall goals. (Robbins, DeCenzo & Coulter, 2015)

The HOW:

There are many things to consider as you think about developing a sports and recreation ministry in your church. There are key questions to ask related to the broad understanding sport ministers should consider related to a ***strategic plan*** process or Building Blocks to put into place, fundamentals for success to contemplate, and pitfalls to avoid. So let us break these key elements down when it comes to building a vibrant and impactful Sports and Recreation Ministry and walk through what each of them are about.

The Key Questions:

If you are going to build a vibrant and impactful sports and recreation ministry in your church (or anywhere else for that matter), then we have to begin by asking some key questions. I believe that by asking and answering these questions we can then begin to put together a strategic plan for building a ***successful*** sports and recreation ministry in your church. Preview the questions here, discuss them with your colleagues, but know now, that these same questions will be asked of you at the end of this chapter and you should write out responses to get the benefit of progressing through your sports ministry.

Success is a variable term, success is what you, the sport minister makes it, but it needs to be identified early with measurable components, and should be a part of the story you tell.

Everything else you do from here on out in building and establishing a sports and recreation ministry will be determined by the answers to these questions. Also, do not be afraid to ask others to come alongside and too join you in the journey as you seek to find the answers. So here are those questions:

1. What sports or activities are hot in your community?

2. What activities are not being offered by other churches or sport ministries in the area?

3. What activities would be easy to promote, implement, and draw people in?

4. What are your available resources? (Christian & Secular/Facilities, Financial, and People)

5. If we could do only one activity and do it well, what would it be?

6. Who will be on the leadership team?

7. Are there any legal issues that need consideration?

Legal issues are an important aspect to consider. There are many aspects in running a sports ministry that fall under legal issues including risk management, premise liability and negligence to name a few. Further investigation in to these terms is necessary.

Some examples of secondary questions concerning ***legal issues*** to consider might be the following...

a) Does your church have any type of insurance release form that maybe another ministry is already using that you could format for you sports and recreation ministry participants, or do you need to work with a lawyer in your church to create one?

b) Do you have the proper insurance coverage on your facilities and the people that use your facilities for this type of programming?

The Building Blocks:

Once we have asked and answered the key questions (see the learning-to-action section at the end of this chapter to answer these questions) it is time to start putting in the Building Blocks for your ministry. There are two types of Building Blocks you need to establish:

Foundational Building Blocks—These are the non-negotiables, if you will. These are the Building Blocks in which everything in your ministry will be based on and filtered through.

Supportive Building Blocks—how the ministry looks, is implemented and how it functions.

Three Foundational Building Blocks:

1. Vision/Prayer – We want to begin by sincerely seeking after God and His direction for our ministry. We want to make sure this is a "God Thing!"

Goals are the desired outcomes or targets for your sports ministry.

2. Goal setting – We want to make sure as we begin to build and establish strategy for our ministry that will include stretching but reasonable ***goals*** for everything we are doing. This includes leadership and the breadth of program development, timing of the startup of programming etc....

3. Leadership – Pray for God to guide you to the "right" leaders. Establishing the right leadership structure, with the right leaders in the right places on the bus will go a long way in building a successful ministry. (See Chris Phillips chapter for more about Leadership and leadership development)

Once you have established the Foundational Building Blocks, the next step is to lay the Supportive Building Blocks. These are the blocks that help you put everything together in partnership with one another within your program, as you will see, in order to build an effective and impactful ministry.

Three Supportive Building Blocks:

1. Compatibility – How will what you are planning to establish in your ministry mesh with the other ministries of your church, with your people, with your community?

2. Environment – What will be the ***environment***? Stand alone, or a part of something else, another ministry of the church, a partnership in the community?

Environments are forces that effect your sports ministry performance both internally and externally.

3. Leadership – A successful and effective sports and recreation ministry has multiple layers of volunteer leadership.

NOTE: You may have noticed that I think there is an important need in both the Foundational and Supportive Building Blocks for strong leadership. In case you are a bit confused here, it really is all about developing external leadership and internal leadership. Now that we have answered some key questions, and established some very important and strategic building blocks there are some fundamentals for success that we need to take a look at. To build a successful sports and recreation ministry there are three fundamental points we always need to be aware of.

1. "Mission Driven" leadership

To build a successful Sports and Recreation Ministry we must always make sure that we are guided by the mission. That mission, however you want to paint it, is ultimately about redeeming the world for the Kingdom's sake. Jesus understood this, and had great conviction about the mission. Everything He did came back to the mission. Here are just a couple of examples…

As Jesus went on from there, he saw a man named Matthew sitting at the tax collector's booth. "Follow me," he told him, and Matthew got up and followed him. While Jesus was having dinner at Matthew's house, many tax collectors and "sinners" came and ate with him and his disciples. When the Pharisees saw this, they asked his disciples, "Why does your teacher eat with tax collectors and 'sinners'?" On hearing this, Jesus said, "It is not the healthy who need a doctor, but the sick. But go and learn what this means: 'I desire mercy, not sacrifice.' For I have not come to call the righteous, but sinners." (Matthew 9:9-13)

When Jesus reached the spot, he looked up and said to him, "Zacchaeus, come down immediately. I must stay at your house today." 6 So he came down at once and welcomed him gladly. 7 All the people saw this and began to mutter, "He has gone to be the guest of a 'sinner.'" But Zacchaeus stood up and said to the Lord, "Look, Lord! Here and now I give half of my possessions to the poor, and if I have cheated anybody out of anything, I will pay back four times the amount." Jesus said to him, "Today salvation has come to this house, because this man, too, is a son of Abraham. For the Son of Man came to seek and to save what was lost." (Luke 19:5-10)

Here is the bottom line when it comes to building a successful Sports and Recreation Ministry. Follow Christ's example, Jesus did not come to run programs, but to seek and save the lost!!

2. Advanced planning & preparation. *(Especially the ministry).* Advanced planning and preparation are such an important aspect of building a successful ministry. Everything that we present to those who will participate in our ministries and I mean everything must be done right and with excellence. If we are going to stay close to the mission God has called our ministry too, then the ministry in our programs matter, and that just does not happen by accident. If we want to engage people with the Gospel we have got to make sure that we are purposeful in doing so. As much or more effort needs to be put into developing the ministry components of our programing as anything else. We sometimes can get so wrapped up in the marketing and promotion of our programs, the training of volunteers, schedules, team selections, facilities, and equipment that we forget what matters most. And, that is the development of the ministry components that will ultimately engage the hearts of our participants and bring transformation to their lives.

3. Different approaches for different programs.

When developing your ministry, you need to always keep in mind that every program is different from the other, and should be treated as such. For example, Youth Basketball, Men's Flag Football, and Cycling classes are all completely different from one another. They will draw in different people and will have their own unique set of circumstances, especially when it comes to developing the ministry aspect of these programs.

When it comes to different approaches for different programs, everything must be evaluated; including promotion and marketing, recruitment of volunteers, length of programing, age appropriate devotional material, etc....

Do your homework and you can develop a very diverse and impactful ministry!

The Top (7) reasons as to why sports & recreation ministries are not successful:

Just as there are reasons sports and recreation ministries are successful, there are many reasons why they are not.

1. Not First Class

No matter what the size or breadth of your program if it is not first class in its set up and implementation you will not be able to build a sustainable and impactful ministry.

2. Inadequate Finances

We have got to make sure that we are resourcing our ministry adequately. It does not mean that you have to have unlimited resources to be successful, it simply means that you must make sure that you have the necessary resources in place to run an effective ministry. Make a plan, itemize potential expenses…it does not take a lot of financial resources, but some is necessary.

3. Lack of Support *(Internal and External)*

If you do not have adequate support from church leadership, volunteers, participants, the church family, and the community you will always be facing an uphill battle. You must continually cultivate support to ensure your ministry stays vibrant and impactful. Start with getting one of each on board.

4. No Ministry Emphasis

This may sound like a no-brainer, but making sure that the ministry emphasis is always at the forefront of what your program is offering is critical to the impact on the lives your ministry will have on your participants. Always remember that ministry does not just happen, it must be purposefully planned into the DNA of your programming.

5. Narrow Focus

If you are too narrow focused in your programming, there is a good chance you will miss out on opportunities to reach those in your church and/or community. It is all about finding the balance between doing too little and trying to do too much.

6. Members Unwilling to Serve

As the ministry leader you are the vision caster, the recruiter, the trainer, the inspirer of those who could potentially be involved in your ministry. Some may be unwilling to serve. Just know that this happens, it is not you, but it is often a results of members being afraid of change. Keep delivering the message…keep delivering the Good News!

7. Facilities

You can have a well-respected and life impacting sports and recreation ministries with or without owning your own facilities. The reason ministries suffer is that they do not have the proper facilities for the activities and programs they are offering. Making sure you have the proper facilities for your programming is key to building a successful one. If an issues of facilities are a problem, I encourage you to take a close look at Reverend Joe Smith (Chapter 2) and David Waddell (Chapter 8).

Conclusion

As I wrap up my section of this chapter, my prayer is that you can see just how special and impactful a sports and recreation ministries can be for you and your church. Sports and recreation ministries can change how our churches view reaching our communities and our world. It can also be the tool that God uses to impact our communities to a greater extent than almost anything else we may think to do.

Sports and recreation ministry can change how our churches view reaching our communities and our world. It can also be the tool that God uses to impact our communities to a greater extent than almost anything else we may think to do, but to do that it must be (3) things…

INTENTIONAL!! – RELATIONAL!! – INVITATIONAL!!

Learning-to-action exercise

1. What activities are hot in our community and amongst our people?

____

____

2. What activities are not being offered by others?

____

____

3. What activities would be easy to promote, implement, and draw people in?

____

____

4. What are your available resources? (Christian & Secular / Facilities, Financial, and People)

____

____

5. If we could do only one activity and do it well, what would it be?

____

____

6.Are there any legal issues that need consideration?

____

____

PART 2 – RELATIONAL

Simple and organic sports ministry through forming relationships: Pray – Play – Say

Steve Quatro
Executive Director
Sports Outreach, Los Angeles
Professor – Azusa Pacific University
Former CSRM Board of Trustees and Staff Member

After hearing about or observing large church sports ministry endeavors, have you ever been discouraged because you think our church can never do that? Church sports do not have to be big to be effective. I have learned a lot from my wonderful colleagues who God has used to develop and run large church sports ministries. And I am convinced God is using their efforts to bring many into an eternal relationship with Jesus Christ. Large church sports ministries do wonderful and effective work for God's glory and to build His Kingdom. Praise God! Whether you are in a large or small church, however, the perspective of this chapter takes a look at the strategic bridge of sports that connects saved and lost people. The ways of this chapter and others chapters in this handbook can be employed in simple and organic ways that are very effective.

Can a church that has no sports facilities (or no facilities at all!), no staff dedicated to sports ministry, no budget to allocate, still employ the greatest bridge to share the Greatest Story Ever Told? I shout a loud "Yes they can!" While several chapters in this handbook will provide insights from great sport ministers from around the country in relation to starting a ministry or building a ministry, this chapter is truly foundational from a relational perspective. This chapter can help either those that want to start a sports ministry or those that have a sports ministry and need to take a step back and gain perspective of their sports ministry. I will share ways that I believe a church can very simply and organically employ sports (or virtually any leisure activity) to build relationships of trust with people who do not yet call Jesus Christ their Savior.

Relationships of trust

Trust is certainly relational (as Steve describes in this chapter, but it is also managerial, suggesting that trust is an attribute many employees and coaches feel all leaders should have to be successful. Beenis and Goldsmith (2013) and Scott (2014) identify four "ingredients" for creating trust:

1. Competency
2. Congruity
3. Constancy
4. Caring

See the end of this chapter for definitions.

What do I mean by relationships of ***trust***? From my perspective, distrust and antagonism toward anything Christian or Biblical is increasing in America at an accelerating and scary rate. This makes it extremely difficult to have a meaningful conversation about Jesus Christ without it quickly escalating into a Facebook-like rant. However, if believers and non-believers could develop relationships where there is a growing trust of each other, the discussions could occur without the expectation of antagonism. Without this relationship of trust spiritual discussions usually move in toward those places where people disagree. When there is a foundation of trust, the discussion can focus on Jesus and the Good News instead of becoming antagonistic. So, how does this relate to church sports ministry? Let me briefly describe three reasons a church should consider employing sports.

1. Sports are a tremendous bridge to facilitate the developing of relationships.

"Sports are the greatest bridge to lost people." This is how Senior Pastor Mike Schoonover of Glendora Community Church in California describes the value of sports in building relationships with people outside his church. He incorporated pick-up soccer in a local park in the rebirthing of his church. Observing whom advertisers involve to endorse and sell their products can see an indication of the power of sports in America.

2. Sports can bridge the divisions that make it difficult to have meaningful conversations with people we desire to reach; whether those divisions are racial, political, cultural, or economic.

This is especially important given the rising antagonism to the Bible and Christianity that I mentioned above. The relationships of trust made through sports allow spiritual conversations to take place without that antagonism.

3. Sports will allow you to build deeper relationships more quickly than most other points of contact.

Erik Thoennes, Talbot Seminary Professor and former NCAA football player, believes that "sports accelerates the building of relationships." The winning and losing, being on a team, seeing the wonder of nature together, pushing yourself to your physical limits together, getting injured and recovering—all of these experiences done with others accelerates the deepening of relationships.

I believe the highest and best use of sports and recreation through a local church is the bridge it provides to those who do not attend church. This bridge can be utilized to develop relationships of trust that can lead to, when appropriate, prayerfully sharing with people the wonder of Jesus.

In summary, engaging in sports and recreation activities regularly with others will allow the building of relationships of trust. These relationships will provide the bridge to engage in spiritual conversations across the divisions and antagonism that typically keep these eternal conversations from happening. What a tremendous opportunity!

Sports and recreation activities can be employed simply and organically to build relationships of trust with the people God is calling you to reach. The three principles below will help you build relationships of trust with people who can then, in a very natural way, see and hear the Gospel.

Principle 1: Develop intentional and specific prayer.

Prayer is critical to any endeavor for which we want to see eternal results—it is even more important when the endeavor is evangelistic in its focus. Paul pleaded with the Colossians in chapter 4 to devote themselves to prayer for himself and his co-workers because they were sharing the Gospel. He asks them to pray for:

1. An open door to share the message (Col. 4:3).
2. God to give clarity when proclaiming the message (Col. 4:4).

3. Wisdom when dealing with outsiders (Col. 4:5).
4. The blessing of making the most of every opportunity (Col. 4:5).
5. Their conversation to be full of grace and seasoned with salt so they know how to answer everyone (Col. 4:6).

It is critical that you develop a team of people who will regularly ask God to guide and bless your efforts; and you do this BEFORE you go out and play with lost people. This requires far more than circling up and praying after you play a game or go on a hike. Even in the simplest and most organic sports ministry, prayer is essential to seeing eternal results.

In addition to Paul's list above, your prayer team could also ask God for:

1. Wisdom to know what sports or activities to play. Think, people first—whom are you trying to reach? The sport/activity is secondary.

2. Where and when to engage in the activity—this may determine who comes.

3. The Holy Spirit to draw those He wants to participate—not just sports all-stars from the church.

4. Physical protection from injuries.

5. Self-control of those participating—especially the believers playing.

6. Protection from the enemy of the God and His work in the world (see Ephesians 6:10-20).

7. Key volunteers. When Jesus was in Jerusalem, He looked over the people of His city with compassion and gave the disciples a task—pray for laborers (Matthew 9:36-38). Employing sports to reach out does not require a lot of volunteers, but

they do need to be the right ones—those drawn by God's Spirit. So ask God for them – like Jesus told us to.

8. His guidance in developing relationships of trust with the participants of your sports activities.

And the Survey Says...

When completing my Master's thesis at Biola University in Southern California I surveyed 94 churches that employed sports for ministry purposes. I hired a professional statistician to analyze the survey data. His purpose was to determine which aspect of the churches' sports ministry (e.g., church size, facilities, paid staff, Senior Pastor support, sports ministry budget, etc.) correlated most closely to families becoming engaged in the life of the church (through the bridge of the sports ministry). Intentional and specific prayer was greater than two times more likely to be correlated to families joining the church than any other aspect! Two times more likely! Invest in prayer.

Do not overlook the importance and strategic advantage prayer brings to incorporating sports in your church outreach efforts. You will have to invest time to ask people to pray, then give them specifics for which to pray; but if you desire eternal results you must ask God to work. So, develop intentional and specific prayer for your sports outreach efforts.

Principle 2: Develop relationships of trust with lost people.

Employing the bridge of sports to build relationships of trust with lost people is most effective when keeping a few core values in mind.

1. Keep the main thing the main thing. Building relationships with lost people, or those not attending a Christ-magnifying church, needs to be a primary goal of employing sports in this endeavor. Sports ministry, even when done with the best intentions, can lose sight of its purpose if it is not monitored. If you do not keep the focus on developing new relationships with people in your community, your sports activity can easily slide into merely a place where Christians play games with other Christians. When this happens church sports can easily become, as one senior pastor told bad sports, bad ministry, and me.

2. Behave! Remember our prayer above to make the most of every opportunity and to let our conversation be full of grace seasoned with salt? This does not include arguing with the ref or with an opponent. It NEVER, EVER includes retaliating. Remember our prayer for God to bring us the right volunteers? If you are the person who typically "loses it" in a competitive situation remove yourself from the sports ministry and serve in another ministry at your church. It is far better to lose a game graciously because of a ref's bad calls or an opponent's hard fouls than to complain or retaliate. When you compete well without complaining or retaliating you will be building relationships of trust. The participants watching will be more likely to listen to you share about Jesus when they see you get fouled and not retaliate or complain. Not easy but impacting. So, behave and see Chapter 9 of this handbook to learn ways to manage conflict.

3. Value people over sports. Another way to build relationships of trust is to be ready and willing to stop the activity to minister to someone who is injured or has a need that requires your attention. And yes, this applies even if you are winning in the last inning of the softball game! When others are all about winning, being focused on people leaves a mark—In a good way. Be OK with being outscored in a game. If you are always winning the game, people will doubt your motives. If you are playing in a competitive arena, play hard and to the best of your ability, but losing is not a bad thing. For example, adding the automatic out to your softball team roster shows you value people over the score—that is a way to let your conversation be full of grace and seasoned with salt. So, value people over sports.

4. Choose your activity wisely. In my 2009 book *Intentional Outreach,* I recommended to churches that they develop activities that encourage significant conversations. Here are a few suggestions to help make that happen (not gospel, just suggestions).

a. When playing a competitive, body-to-body, sport (e.g., basketball or soccer) recruit committed Christians who support the purpose of the activity to make up about 50% of the participants. Remember, the purpose is not to outscore the other team. The goal is build relationships of trust that will allow meaningful conversations to happen. If the activity gets too physical and heated the ability to hear the Good News of love and grace will be diminished.

b. Coed sports lead to more significant conversations than sports with all male participants. Do not shoot the messenger (me), this is what I have observed in 20 plus years of working with church leaders in sports outreach. I am not saying that all sports need to be coed, but coed sports typically lead to deeper relationships and more significant conversations.

c. You do not need to own a gym. If your simple and organic sports activity grows and you need something more formal you can rent parks or school gyms. Running, hiking and biking do not require church-owned facilities. Sand volleyball can be played at the beach for free. Lost people in your community play games in parks and rec centers, go play with them. There is nothing wrong with owning sports facilities, but to employ sports for simple and organic outreach, facilities are not necessary. See Chapter 8 in this handbook that discusses running a sports ministry with limited space.

d. Organize the activity so you have ongoing contact (e.g., every Saturday morning games or hikes) as opposed to a one-time event. Do not underestimate the relational equity built up by playing a game or hiking with someone week after week after week after… Building relationships of trust requires spending time together, therefore organize your activities so you spend ongoing time together.

e. Organize the activity so it leads into spontaneous conversations. Plan to stay after the game is over to talk; or arrange an after-activity meal. The conversations at these times are very valuable. Playing with or against someone, then spending an hour with them over a meal will yield significant conversations. Sport accelerates the building of relationships.

So, choose your activity wisely.

Below are additional strategies that can be used quite simply to meet new people and build relationships of trust.

• On a Saturday morning or weekday evening go to a park and get into an age- and skill-appropriate soccer, basketball, ultimate Frisbee, etc. game and start making friends. Keep going back at the same time and place. Do not forget that the goal is to develop relationships. After the game spend time with those to whom the Holy Spirit is leading you.

• If you have enough people, join a coed or single gender community league. Cities, rec centers, and YMCAs offer softball, basketball, soccer, volleyball, hiking, biking, and running/fitness clubs. A few people already associated with your church can prayerfully invite others who need to hear the Gospel to join the team.

Do not join a league in which local churches play against other churches. This competition among believers, which sadly turns ugly in many cases, is hard for the unbelievers on your team to get past this sort of conflict.

• Get six or more people, go to a park on Saturday morning with some simple soccer goals and a soccer ball, and start playing soccer (this works with volleyball also). When you see people watching, invite them to play. Mix up the teams—do not try to show the world that the people from your church can beat all comers. Keep going to the same location at the same time every week. The nice thing about doing this, as opposed to the first method listed above, is that because it is your equipment, you have a little control. This control can be very strategic because you can end the game and transition into organic and significant conversations.

The three methods above will most likely require some scouting and prayer trips to see where, when, and what people are playing. Do not try to start too many activities at once; start with one activity and do it well. Then, if God leads and provides more key volunteers, add other strategic activities to meet even more people.

Principle 3: Intentionally and thoughtfully share with lost people about God.

In a "typical" church sports ministers' training, significant time is spent on this principle—that is, how to appropriately share with the participants about God. However, in the simple and organic settings described in this chapter, the conversations are more natural—as opposed to a "God talk" at halftime of a game. "God talks" connected to a sports / rec activity can be very effective in setting the stage to have significant individual conversations. However, in less formal activities, when the participants may not have registered with you or your church to play in a league, it can be awkward to transition from the game to a "talk" about God. These spiritual and eternally important conversations can happen in a simpler and more natural way. The below ideas along with Chapter 3 show a great combination of information to get the conversation started and share the Good News with believers and non-believers alike.

1. Train ALL your volunteers involved with the sports activity to be able to clearly and appropriately share the Gospel. Someone as bold and experienced as the Apostle Paul asked the Colossians to pray that he would share the message boldly and clearly. Paul knew that he could improve. Even if a volunteer does not think she / he will be the one to share the Gospel, God has a way of arranging His own timetable and setting for significant conversations to happen. God may desire for a lost person to hear the Gospel from someone who needs to step out in faith to boldly share it. Lost people sometimes see another participant in the sports / rec activity as more credible than someone who gets paid (aka, a church staff member) to tell people about God. This is even more impacting if they have observed the volunteer competing well (see Principle 2).

2. Encourage every volunteer to look for opportunities to engage in a conversation that go deeper than the game / activity; and to seek the leading of God's Spirit and boldly follow His leading. Sometimes God may be leading your volunteers to address a specific question a person asks while leaving other topics for a later time.

Consider leaving a seeker wanting to talk again, instead of wishing they had never asked anything about God. For example, when someone suggests that everyone get together to play again on Sunday morning you could respond with something like, "Oh, I would love to play again but a few years ago my life was heading in a really bad direction and I learned some things that completely turned my life around. On Sundays I get to hang out with people who helped me back then, and help keep me focused now." If you stop at that point, the person will probably ask you for more information. They asked about playing on Sunday and you answered why you do not. They did not ask (yet!) about your faith in God. Pray that God's Spirit will keep bringing your comments to their mind until they ask again. Remember the suggestion above to plan ongoing activities so you have regular contact.

3. When God privileges you to have the opportunity to share the Gospel with someone, focus on Jesus. Start with where people are but focus on Jesus. Do not let the cultural hot topic of the day dominate the conversation. Jesus is amazing, tell people about Him and how the Lord has effected your life.

4. As God draws people to salvation be ready with a "next step" activity to which you can invite people. Not all church gatherings are appropriate for new believers or those God is drawing. If your church does not offer a new believers Bible study (or something similar), consider starting one. It can start as a short-term easily accessible gathering with a clearly stated purpose. For example, if you have one person who has newly trusted in Christ and one who is very interested in learning more, you can find a time the two of them can meet with a mature Christian (hopefully involved in the sports activity). Then invite others to join you, stating the purpose—"John, Joe and I are going to grab lunch for the next four Saturdays after we play to learn more about Jesus and what it means to believe in Him. We would love to have anyone else interested join us."

Trust in God's Spirit to do the work of conversion. Be faithful, loving, and clear in your witness of the mercy and eternal life offered through Jesus. Our role is to faithfully "go, make, and teach" (Matthew 28:18-20), it is God's job to do the work of conversion. Persevere. Be prepared to keep serving for the long term. Paul encourages Timothy to do the work of an evangelist—it is work. Play regularly with lost people using the guidelines included above and God will use the relationships of trust that He is building to do His eternal work.

I have heard other sports ministers summarize the above principles this way.

1. Pray: Pray intentionally and specifically for God to use your efforts to save lost people.
2. Play: Play with lost people in a way that they see Christ in you.
3. Say: Say something. When God opens the door to have a spiritual conversation, be bold and loving in your witness.

I pray that God will bless you richly as you simply and organically employ the bridge of sports to build relationships of trust with people, and that you have the privilege of sharing the Good News of salvation in Jesus.

Chapter 1 – Part 2 Definitions

Bennis and Goldsmith (2013) and Scott (2014) offer "ingredients" for creating trust:

1. Competence: Followers must believe that leaders are capable of doing their job.
2. Congruity: Associated with integrity. What a leader says is congruent with what he/she does.
3. Constancy: Followers want leaders who are on their side, who will support and defend them.
4. Caring: A leader cares about the lives of followers and cares about the implications of actions and decisions that affect them.

Learning-to-action exercise

1. What are some specific things for which you will ask people to pray in relation to your sports and recreation ministry?

____

____

2. How can you keep these prayer partners engaged as you reach out through sports?

____

____

3. What group of people would you like to reach using sports and/or recreation activities?

____

____

4. Where might you find this group of people engaging in these activities?

____

____

5. Who from your church can you invite to join you when you play with these people?

____

____

6. What appropriate next step activity can you invite those who are interested?

____

____

CHAPTER TWO

POSSIBILITIES

for Sport Ministry in a Small Church

Rev. Joe BW Smith
St. John's Lutheran Church
Lakewood, WA
@youravgpastor

Proclaimed reasons for small churches not to do sport ministry—and why you may hear them

"We can't do what First Mega Church does! They're so big. They have a huge budget and a large staff! We only have volunteers, and those volunteers are stretched too thin already."

"Community Church has a beautiful new gym! My nephew and his friends go over there every Monday night for open gym basketball, and they love that they can hang out there. We don't have any kind of space like that, and even the building we have needs a lot of repair."

"Our church is small; the members we do have are older. We have a few kids, but not even enough to have a Sunday School. We don't have the programs to attract families with children, so we don't know what to do."

Over 80% of all church attenders in the United States will worship each Sunday in a congregation with an average weekend attendance of 100, but many of these churches have far less in attendance (Chart of National Congregation Study, 2010). A majority of U.S. Congregations are small congregations, often with limited staff and **resources**. Is it possible for a small church to engage in sport ministry?

For an organization **Resources** are all assets, capabilities, attributes, information and knowledge controlled by the organization. Resources are considered tangible (such as a facility) or intangible such as the sport ministry culture, reputation, and motivation of coaches and participants. *(Chelladurai, 2005)*

In my experience in teaching, consulting, and pastoring small congregations for two decades, they frequently compare themselves to large congregations, and often feel a sense of inferiority about their ministry in the community. The sample statements above reflect some of the comparisons small church members make when reflecting upon their ministry. Small churches are involved in good and important ministry. At a small church, there is often a sense of familiarity, family, and home. They may have a Bible study or two, a small Sunday school, seasonal fellowship events, an outreach to serve those in need, or a vacation Bible school. The idea of sport ministry is likely beyond their imagination, especially in congregations where most of the attenders are senior citizens. If the congregation has been in decline, sport ministry represents a memory of a more glorious past, which brings a different sense of resistance to the idea of sport ministry.

One small congregation's story regarding sport ministry

I currently serve a congregation, St. John's Lutheran Church in Lakewood, Washington, that once had a more glorious past. The current average Sunday attendance is about 50, up from 5 years ago when it was about 25 and pondering permanently closing its doors. Over a decade ago, the attendance was over 100 per Sunday. St. John's had an energetic Sunday school, vacation Bible school, and a youth group. There were numerous social activities, a choir, and many opportunities to serve those in need. A variety of factors contributed to their decline, but when faced with the prospect of closing the church and selling the property—with the help of judicatory staff and volunteers supporting the remaining members, God worked with St. John's to imagine a new future. Whereas the attitude was hopeful, there was still lament about a history that was lost, and the church faced stark realities about the present. The Sunday school had closed years ago. There were no kids in the congregation (until my two kids tagged along). Why would a family with children even come to St. John's when they had nothing to offer them? Sport ministry in the small church may not save a small church from extinction, but the opportunities of sport ministry for the small church may change the attitude and approach of that congregation that can provide a foundation to thrive.

A brief primer on Protestant denominational history in the United States and that history's effect on variables related to a small church

One of the contributing variables to church decline in the United States is the church's understanding of mission. Loren Meade's (1991) *The Once and Future Church* chronicles the mission and purpose understanding of Christian churches in the 18th through 20th centuries. During those centuries, churches were frequently organized around municipalities, ethnicities, and/or denominational subcultures. Church was a place that particular people gathered, almost always homogeneous. In order to be a good Christian and good citizen, one participated in worship services, supported religious education and relationships in the home and/or church, and contributed to mission in far off lands. Mission happened away from the church. Household and congregations contributed to support missionaries in Africa, Asia, and South America, including Bible translators so that people could read the Bible in their own language, a product of the Protestant Reformation some 200-400 years earlier. Mission was far away, not nearby, because almost every connection in one's own sphere of influence was related to some ***faith community***. As this tide slowly changed in the 20th century, many churches failed to recognize that mission opportunities were also nearby, as demographic profiles (i.e., age and race) of cities and neighborhoods changed with new waves of immigration and other demographic variable influences. Even then, the church growth and Evangelical movements of the mid to late 20th century championed church growth through an attractional understanding, much like in the movie *Field of Dreams*. In this movie, the key phrase being interpreted throughout the film is, "If you build it, he will come." At the climax of the movie, a child sees that if something that people want to be a part of is built, people will come. The fortunes of the family and the entire community will change for the better. A church that

A **faith community** is a group of people that share the same religious beliefs.

seeks to fulfill an inspirational vision will often see things the in a *Field of Dreams* kind of way—if we build a beautiful new building with inspirational programs for everyone in the family, people will come, and often come quickly (Thumma & Bird, 2015).

In the attraction understanding Christian mission, a downside can be that the congregation becomes self-centered, building for its own concerns and needs. If a small church drifts toward self-centeredness in the past 30 years, that behavior will lead to closure, if it has not happened already. Closure does not mean that the church was lacking good ministry, or that somehow God was not at work in that place. However, the conditions that produced the church of the 18th through 20th centuries that allowed a congregation to focus on a narrow demographic no longer exist in their entirety.

Even though St. John's Lutheran Church began to see a better future in the first two years of its turnaround, the congregation still lamented the paucity of children. What could be done to bring children in? Critical mass and program start-up costs are limited. Why would families with children come?

An alternative to an attractional understanding of church, and its foundation for sport ministry in a small church

Mission does not have to follow attractional understanding or be in a far off place, but in our own neighborhood. My teacher, Luther Seminary Professor Pat Keifert often told me and my colleagues, "People don't care what you know until they know that you care." (P. Keifert, personal communication, April 28, 1998). With that in mind, meeting people where they are becomes the relationship building opportunity, rather than waiting for people to come to the church.

Churches that were formed and built between the 18th and 20th centuries often carry something similar to their original DNA . That is, for my own tradition in the Lutheran Church, congregations during those centuries frequently formed based on ethnic identities in North America—from Northern European countries, Norway, Sweden, Finland, Denmark, and Germany. These Northern European immigrants came to the United States full of opportunities, but also full of hardships and disorientation from monumental change. The church was identified as something from the home country, and it resisted change (Kiefert, 1994). The church was a place of comfort and safety. For many churches founded under those conditions, the idea of actively meeting neighbors of different socio-economic backgrounds and ethnicities, and building community with them in a congregation seemed contrary to their origins. This is not unique to the Lutheran Church; it is a common pattern for 1st and 2nd generation immigrant communities, whether from Europe, Asia, or South America.

Crafting a small church sport ministry

For the small church with limited resources, how to invest in a sport ministry is critical. The best chance for impact is to discover the convergence of interest in a few of the congregation's members, and a need in the neighborhood. In 1973 Christian author Frederick Beuchner wrote, "The place God calls you to is the place where your deep gladness and the world's deep hunger meet" (Buechner, 2013). Where is that meeting of hunger and gladness for your church? For example, if the church is a neighbor to a middle school, a sport ministry could be as simple as a group of congregational members choosing to adopt a particular sport team and commit to attending their home games. A group of people from Second Baptist Church becomes part of the fan base of the Central Middle School Girls' Volleyball Team—maybe parents of the players are working during the games and cannot attend; attending becomes a chance for kids to know that their efforts matter. Rather than just dropping in to a volleyball match, a few of the interested church members could meet with someone at the school connected with athletics and say, "how can we show support for your student athletes?"

Lakewood, Washington, is an urban environment with high transience due to poverty and/or military families. Basketball is the highest youth participation sport in the United States, with some of the highest sport participation rates among lower income brackets (Lee, 2015). With an opportunity to sponsor youth basketball, St. John's Lutheran Church helped support a Kindergarten-1st grade co-ed basketball team through the municipal parks and recreation department. The church provided a $175 sponsorship, which helped cover scholarships for families who

[2] Churches do not have genetic codes per se, but DNA can be a metaphor for discussing the origins of your church, including history, understanding of mission, past pastors and/or staff members, prominent congregational leaders, etc.

could not afford for their child to play, uniform shirts, and subsidize pay for referees. I coached the K-1 team with members of the congregation. Other members of the congregation attended games and cheered for kids. St. John's hosted a pizza and ice cream party at the end of the season at the church, with members providing hospitality to players and their families. As a church, we thanked the families for the opportunity to join them in doing something positive in the community, and stating explicitly that community involvement is part of St. John's understanding of being a church in Lakewood. The families were gracious and appreciative. The costs associated with the basketball season amounted to around $400 to the church, which was an affordable opportunity to connect with our community. Even if we did not have the money in our church budget, we would seek to raise the funds to continue that partnership.

Objectives are the stated "stepping stones" to eventually reach stated goals. See end of this chapter for description of SMART goals and objectives

Measuring success in a sport ministry depends on the goals and ***objectives*** your faith community sets. For St. John's and its ongoing congregational redevelopment, trusting relationships in the community are the goal, regardless of whether people who participate in youth basketball come to St. John's for worship or come to Christian faith. Faith and worship are considered good things, but bonuses. The goal in St. John's ministry with youth basketball was to build relationships with community leaders, and relationships with families with children.

What have been key relationships with community leaders? First, there is a positive relationship with the Director of Lakewood Parks and Recreation, Dennis. For example, Dennis was an advocate for St. John's work with youth basketball in a key community strategy meeting with its denomination. Dennis also offered insight to other ways in which St. John's could connect with families through municipal activities. Dennis also has relationships with families who meet at St. John's through a local Boy Scout troop. As a community leader, Dennis has a positive understanding of St. John's and its neighborhood relationships.

Another example of a community relationship—one of the parents of a team member is a retired career Army officer who currently works in placing veterans in meaningful work who have returned from Iraq and Afghanistan. As a Roman Catholic, John was already part of a faith community, but his awareness of St. John's sport ministry was important for local perception of the congregation. Many of John's conversations at practice and games were with a team assistant coach, an active duty Army soldier. They conversed about their shared experience and wisdom about life in the military.

Considering your church's theology and tradition and building community relations

Community is a specific activity designed to foster desirable relationships between your sport ministry and the communities in which it is either located or has strategic interests (Stoldt, Dittmore, & Branvold, 2012).

How does a church connect to individuals, families, and households? There are many facets upon which to reflect. Be aware of your faith community and tradition as you consider your strategy, philosophy, and theology. For example, in my tradition, there is often resistance to explicit invitations to Christian faith. Some traditions are explicit in their intention that they are inviting people to be practicing Christians. Awareness of your theology and philosophy will allow your leadership to create shared goals that challenge and uplift your faith community. Regardless of the theology and philosophy of your church (there are infinite variances), another important consideration for your ministry is the previous level of involvement in community activities by the congregation. Small congregations are rarely self-sufficient, therefore investment in community relations is crucial in building a sport ministry. Regardless of whether your church's theology/philosophy involves implicit or explicit invitations to Christian faith, it is important to invest in a web of relationships that can uphold a strong sense of congregation and community. If your small congregation already has a strong network of community relationships, congratulations! However, some congregations have limited community connections, therefore it takes some brainstorming, creativity, and inspiration. For example, I have encouraged and engaged in personal volunteering in local public schools and organizations, engaging local civil servants, and befriending local merchants. Because congregations have frequently lost or neglected community relationships apart from their own groups, this can take time. It should be noted that it does not take community relationships to start a sport ministry, but in order to build a ministry that thrives in a small congregation, community relationships are essential. Trust is a key companion to any sport ministry, let alone ministry in general.

Sport as "Neutral Space" ministry

Church can often be an intimidating place for an individual or family. It can be challenging to find a good relational match for anyone seeking a community in faith and an opportunity to worship God. Evangelistic and recruiting efforts historically have often been a matter of turf. Door knocking has been an evangelistic strategy by numerous traditions for decades (e.g., Jehovah's Witness, Latter-Day Saints, Evangelism Explosion). This type of strategy involves breaching the home turf of the one(s) living in that space, which can be intimidating for everyone involved. The attractional understanding of church involves a turf breach as well. Every church sees themselves as friendly. Regardless of the local practices of hospitality or even if that church could be truly friendly, each congregation has its written and unwritten rules about congregational life. For example, the danger for anyone coming into a small church is that the new person sits in the place of a long-time member. That member may gladly "allow" that new person to sit in "their" chair or pew, but almost any church member can report that newcomers have ruffled numerous church feathers over the years merely by their coordinate choice of seating.

For a small church, sport ministry is not something to possess or own. A sport ministry does not belong to me, or to its leader. Sport ministry is not my turf. Sport ministry is an opportunity for people in a faith community to meet their neighbors in a neutral, non-threatening space. Whereas it can be a fearful experience to meet a stranger outside of one's own turf, sport is a neutral space that is organized by a shared set of written rules regarding how relationships are governed. Homes or churches usually do not have such rules. One might argue that biblical texts such as the 10 Commandments serve this purpose of written rules, but churches and homes often painfully and easily split based on the interpretation of these biblical texts. Sport provides a set of rules as such that participants either ascribe to the rules, or the relationship cannot continue (if a basketball player chooses not to follow the rules, either that person can be ejected from the game, and / or cause her team to lose). Granted, there are no per-

[3] Evangelism Explosion is a ministry training program built on individual faith sharing. For more information please visit www.evangelismexplosion.org.

fect boundary, neutral space ministries, but the challenge of possible turf wars is mitigated in public space in comparison to home or church. Keifert in his classes often spoke of social dancing serving as a neutral space in decades and centuries past; waltzes, fox trots, jigs, and reels, etc., provided rules of etiquette and patterns that allowed individuals to meet without infringing on the dangers of turf (P. Kiefert, personal communication, December 20, 1995). This is sometimes a concern in smaller congregations; people are often afraid to venture into something new in a small church, lest they "invade someone's turf" or "step on someone's toes."

A biblical text that might inform what it means to encounter a neighbor in neutral space is John 4, the story of Jesus meeting a woman at the well in the heat of the day. This meeting takes place in public, albeit in the heat of the day in the Ancient Near East, a time when no one wants to be carrying a heavy container of water. The encounter does not take place in the woman's home or in the synagogue, where much less (if anything) may have been shared. Even in this well's neutral space, all kinds of social consequences are at stake, including the male-female public interactions, the woman's relational history, and the ethnic group differences of Jesus and the woman. The opportunity for redemption in John 4 is in a neutral space, a public well. For the small church seeking redemption, or seeking the opportunity to live out a calling, sport ministry is an important consideration.

Learning-to-action exercise

Based on the theme of this chapter, working with your individuals inside and outside of your faith community is important, below are opportunities to apply what you learned from this chapter to your current ministry situation. This exercise is to get you going to build and / or enhance your sport ministry.

List 3 direct faith community members you could contact to support the building or enhancement of your sport ministry program.

Name E-mail Phone

1____

2____

3____

List 3 community members (not directly related to your faith community) you could contact to support the building or enhancement of your sport ministry program.

Name E-mail Phone

1____

2____

3____

Call these individuals and introduce them to your story about your faith community and the benefits of building a sport ministry program. Let them know you need their help.

SMART Goals and objectives

In the strategic planning process, goals and long-term objectives are established for a three-to-five year time frame; it is often recommended that these satisfy the criteria known as SMART (specific, measurable, achievable, realistic and time-bound).

SMART Goals and Objective example

I will contact all three community members to schedule a meeting to tell "our story" by July 1, 20XX.

Write two (2) SMART Goals and Objectives here

SMART Goal / Objective #1

____

____

SMART Goal / Objective #2

____

____

CHAPTER THREE

EVANGELISM

and Sport Ministry

Jake Medcalf
Senior Pastor
First Presbyterian Church
Hayward, California
@PastorJakeM

This chapter, and this handbook for that matter, is literally a matter of life and death.

On the surface that might seem a little dramatic, but as I continue I think you will see that it is true. I was asked to write this chapter and give my perspective on Evangelism and Sports Ministry, as for some, it can be hard to start a conversation about someone's faith out of the blue. Yes, this handbook discusses managerial aspects to improve sport ministers and their programs. I think it is clear that we all want to manage our ministries to the best of our ability. We should all strive to be well-rounded sport ministers (I do not think you would be reading this handbook otherwise). Many of you may be wonderful sport ministers that are comfortable with discussing God's Scripture to others, but believe it or not, there are others that are not as comfortable with the topic. If you are strong in delivering His message, I encourage you to use this chapter and help someone with lesser experience that could be lifted up in sharing God's Word. And for those of you that feel your understanding of delivering God's Word could be enhanced, this chapter can shed light on the wonderful future you have in sharing the Good News. Now…it would be easy for me to jump right in and discuss evangelism in a sports ministry context, but to truly absorb these terms it is important to evaluate them, especially for those that may find this topic challenging.

Ministry and sport

We in our American Christian culture get the word "Ministry" from the Greek word diakoneo, meaning "to serve" or douleuo, meaning "to serve as a slave." When we "minister" to others we are to serve them. As followers of Jesus we are to put the needs of others above our own. Jesus Himself made this clear in the Gospel of Matthew.

Not so with you. Instead, whoever wants to become great among you must be your servant, and whoever wants to be first must be your slave—just as the Son of Man did not come to be served, but to serve, and to give his life as a ransom for many. *(Matthew 22:26-28)*

God Himself came in the form of Jesus to minister or to serve. The term Christian means at its most literal "little Christ." We as Christians are to develop the character, compassion, and competency of Jesus and be little Jesus' wherever we go. Therefore, we also are all meant to be ministers. The "ministry" is not simply for those who wear a collar, a robe, have a seminary degree, or look incredibly smart and handsome drinking Starbucks (like me), ministry is for every single person who calls themselves a Christian because it simply means "to serve."

Combine the word ministry with sports and that might become more exciting and attractive for many of us. Sports ministry is the process by which we use sport to serve our community, our neighborhood, our family, our mission, and our friends. Often we make a theological mistake that service/ministry has to be joyless and sacrificial. We have forgotten that God created the world for it to be enjoyed. God created sport and for thousands of years His people have been competing against each other in contests of one kind or another. For the purpose of this Chapter it is important to understand the context of sport. The Council of Europe (2001) defined sport as "all forms of physical activity, which through casual or organized participation, aim at expressing or improving physical fitness and mental well-being, forming social relationships or obtaining results in competitions at all levels" (p. 1).

Many of you have a favorite sport(s). For me it is basketball and golf. I will reorient my schedule to get the chance to do either. I love playing basketball with my friends. The competition is friendly and the banter is entertaining and relatively harmless. I am able to be in community with others and get exercise that my body desperately needs. When my friends and I golf there is almost always some kind of friendly wager on the line. The increase in pressure to make putts or to put a ball in the fairway increases the enjoyment when said task is accomplished. I will also play softball, ultimate Frisbee, surf, run, bike, hike and the list goes on…why? Because they are fun and we are a reflection of Gods joy when we participate in His image.

Imagine this – you can combine the sport you love to serve the God who loves you. You can combine the sport you love with your Christian calling to be a minister or to serve. You can combine the sport you love to literally save and change lives! Really, it's true, and that simple…so, what are you waiting for?

Evangelism and "grilling machines"

Having defined sports ministry briefly let us now turn to ***evangelism***. Many of you might be saying what does evangelism have to do with sports ministry? Or why is that an important conversation to have? There is this incredible moment in Scripture where God Himself in the form of Jesus Christ of Nazareth lays out in a wonderfully simply but yet incredibly difficult command what exactly He wants from us as His people.

Evangelism in its most basic form is love for our neighbor. As you learn to love teammates, community members, neighbors, fellow competitors, and others you eventually have to engage evangelism.

"Teacher, which is the greatest commandment in the Law?" Jesus replied: "'Love the Lord your God with all your heart and with all your soul and with all your mind.'" This is the first and greatest commandment. And the second is like it: 'Love your neighbor as yourself.' All the Law and the Prophets hang on these two commandments." *(Matthew 22:36-40)*

The ultimate command of God is to respond back to His incredible love with love and the second is connected to it. If you study this passage in the original Greek language you will find that you cannot actually separate the two statements "Love God and Love Neighbor" ... they are linked. The entire breadth of Scripture hangs on those two concepts. Your love for God is expressed in your love for neighbor. Now this love eventually takes the form of service or to use our term noted above...ministering.

Before you jump to all kinds of conclusions about the word evangelism or someone who describes themselves as evangelical let us really take a look at what it means. The English word "evangelism" comes from the Greek word euaggelion. Most literally translated in the noun form, euaggelion means: "gospel" or "good news." In the verb form (euaggelizesthai), the meaning of the word changes slightly to "announce" or "bring good news." The evangelist is one who announces GOOD NEWS! Just like all Christians are commanded to be ministers all Christians are commanded to be evangelists. They are asked to share the Good News that God loves the world and has come to save it and not to condemn it. This is to be done joyfully and with enthusiasm and excitement.

In college, my roommate and still good friend to this day brought home this amazing indoor grilling and cooking machine—it was incredible. You could simply throw a frozen piece of chicken onto the machine and it would cook both sides perfectly and drain all the grease out. It was like a small slice of heaven on earth and we told everyone about it. We told our other roommates, our friends, and our family. It was Good News to all college students! We literally felt it was un-loving of us not to share what we had found. If we are to engage in sports ministry and love our community through the vehicle of sports then at some point we must also share the Good News!

You can do this

You and I were created for two things. First, we were created for an intimate, living, breathing relationship with a personable and knowable God. Nothing has given me more joy in working with faith communities and sport ministries in California over the last 15 years of my life than my interactions with my Heavenly Father. He walks with me and talks with me. I know that may sound a little weird; it certainly still does to me having not grown up in a Christian household myself. The problem is that it is absolutely true. This life giving relationship is available for every single person that walks this planet no matter age, race, stage, country, culture, etc.

Second, you were made for a responsibility. God created you for a purpose and that is to take care of the world around you—which would include your fellow humans. Each and every single one of us has gifts and talents given to us by our Creator and we are at our best when those gifts and talents are used to make the world a better and safer place. You were made to Love God and to Love Neighbor. Nothing will bring you more joy.

But wait there is more! God Himself realized that we were struggling as a people with living into our dual purposes of Loving God and Loving Neighbor. We have an inherent ability to think of ourselves first, to think of our own comfort before others, to use and abuse others for our own gain, to look lustfully on the creation for our own purposes. We have an inherent ability to not Love God and to love ourselves more. The Scripture calls it sin. Tim Keller (2008) has a great definition of sin: "Sin is when a good thing becomes the ultimate thing." When we do not put God first in a loving relationship and take care of our neighbors as if they were…we die. We emotionally die, we physically die, and we spiritually die.

The Scripture says the following:

For the wages of sin is death, but the gift of God is eternal life in Christ Jesus our Lord. (Romans 6:23)

Death is the antonym to Jesus. So God Himself came to take the consequences for our human actions and to set us free to love again. This is what He came for:

I have come that they may have life, and have it to the full. (John 10:10)

The Good News is that God came to Earth to redeem all of His people so that today and forever they may have life and life to the full. I, and many others, have experienced this incredible Good News! You and I can live fully into our purpose and literally never taste death of any kind. THAT IS GOOD NEWS! Evangelism is the process of sharing that Good News because you love people and want to serve them. You want them to have this abundant life that you have experienced. It literally is a matter of life and death for individuals.

If you do sports ministry you will end up loving and serving those with whom you play. As part of loving neighbors and just people in general it becomes necessary in the right context and the right space to share the Good News of an abundant and eternal life that is available to all. To not share when asked would simply not be loving or serving.

Sharing the Good News of an abundant and eternal life found through Jesus should always be done in the context of a loving, caring relationship where both parties know that no matter what the decision is (to believe or not) that both parties will remain deeply committed friends and teammates. Everyone on the planet deserves to hear about the abundant life that God offers through an unconditional friendship with another person.

Share the Good News...without an agenda

The challenge that faith communities often encounter can come in the form of loving people with an agenda. For example, faith communities will love and serve people so that they can talk about Jesus or so that they can present information about Jesus. Once you love a person with a SO THAT attached you have actually ceased to love them and have crossed an invisible boundary into manipulation. I hope desperately that all of my teammates, players, assistant coaches, opponents, and team managers meet Jesus in a powerful way like I have and experience eternal and abundant life. But, no matter what they decide about faith I will love them anyway and I will serve them anyway. That must be the underlying foundation behind all healthy evangelism. So let us combine all of the above into life and death!

As much as it pains me to say this (the truth hurts sometimes), the landscape of religion and the faith community itself in America is changing significantly. In a recent 2014 study of more than 35,000 adults conducted by the Pew Research Center for Religion and Public Life the U.S. is becoming less religious. This study indicated that areas that had seen quality growth in church attendance in the past with older adults 10 years ago had seen small increases for some denominations and declines in attendance for other denominations. More importantly, Millennials were found to be far less observant and attending church than their older counterparts. Based on my experience for the past 15 years I would argue that if a faith community is not growing its attendance (or participation) between a 5-10% rate each year than it is actually dying. This dying off could be due to the normal causes of attrition (death, movement, etc.), it's hard to say.

Second, that almost all faith community growth happens via church transfer (even for mega churches). Here is what I mean, most of the new members that churches gather or experience come from migration, dissatisfaction, or a desire to get their kids character developed. Those are almost all folks who have previously

[4] Details from the Pew Research Center study can be found at http://www.pewforum.org/2015/11/03/u-s-public-becoming-less-religious/

experienced church in some way, shape, or form. They are not primarily people who have grown up outside of a faith community environment (like me). By far the majority of people experience life in a non-faith community environment and if the church does not learn how to announce the Good News of an abundant and eternal life in healthy ways—it literally will die. Therefore, sports ministry becomes a powerful vehicle for the survival of the American church. Healthy evangelism happens best in the context of honest, authentic, open, trusting, loving relationships. Another truth is that "church" people primarily end up with their social network full of other "church" people. When this happens Christians who are called to serve, love, and announce the Good News have nobody to actually announce to.

Sports ministry has the potential to impact all of the above. It is widely known that one of the best unifying forces in the world is a ball. Sports ministry creates the relationships that are necessary for healthy evangelism to take place. I am beyond proud of all the amazing work that the faith community that I am a part of is doing in this arena. We currently run a community based basketball league in partnership with another church for over hundreds of kids from the community. This creates all kinds of amazing relationships that allow for God to interact with folks. We currently have a softball team full of people who do not normally attend church and the conversations have been life giving and hopeful. We currently run two basketball open gyms with over 40 people in attendance each week. We host and participate in a basketball league with over 70 people.

We are starting to see folks from all of these different places become involved with our faith community in ever increasing ways. They have attended worship for the first time, Bible studies, Men's and Women's retreats to name a few. This is all possible by sharing the Good News.

Summary

I could provide you with a step-by-step process that would help you begin your journey as a sport minister and beginning to speak the Good News. Steps can be great…for certain things, but I think offering steps here, in this context, would defeat the purpose and underlying message of this chapter…having an agenda. Steps are a form of an agenda, and steps may not work for evangelism and sports ministry every time. However, I can provide you with a few tips to get you going.

Quick & practical tips for evangelism and sports ministry

Just do It – If there is something that combines the sport you love with serving your community—DO IT!! Start that hiking group, start that walking group, start that softball team and recruit church members and friends. It does not have to start big or perfect—God is not enamored with being big or perfect. Recently my good friend Carter took me Frisbee golfing, I had never been before. Honestly, I was absolutely terrible at it but had a really good time. While we were Frisbee golfing. I encouraged Carter to start inviting people to join him on a regular basis both from our church and from outside the church. No need for an agenda, just gather and enjoy relationships, exercise, and the sport. Carter took that encouragement to heart and has begun to gather folks—sometimes as many as 10. He just DID IT!! Carter is not a Pastor, Carter is not a theologian, Carter is not particularly dynamic, but Carter is a great guy who loves well and invited people to do something he loved—and all of a sudden sports ministry has happened!!

Train – train your people to love well. St Francis of Assisi said the following "Share the Gospel (evangelism) at all times and when necessary use words" (Harris, Chrisman, Sullivan, & Magehee, 1998). It is critically important that people love others with no agenda but are also prepared to provide an answer for the hope they have and for that moment that is coming when they are asked to share about Jesus.

On our church softball team, we have a pitcher who generally does not attend church and / or have a vibrant faith life. The softball team is full of all kinds of folks but definitely a few who walk the walk in regards to Jesus. Recently Chuck's wife passed away unexpectedly due to a heart attack. In his season of grief Chuck had a ton of questions about faith/God/life/death/hope and those amazing folks who had loved Chuck through softball were relationally there to answer and give reasons for the hope they have in Jesus.

Bring the love

While still not as dramatic as I said at the beginning of this chapter, you can see that sports ministry is a matter of life and death—for you, for your friends, and for the faith community, so go out there and share the Good News! Understand what sport, ministry, and evangelism is in your context of your ministry. Once you understand this context, sharing the Good News will be much easier. Bring the love…Bring in God's love to you and emit His love to others without agenda. Speak the Good News the best way you know how. It may be difficult and challenging at first, but the more you do it (just like practicing your favorite sport) the better you will become. As I said when sharing the Good News, "Do it joyfully and with enthusiasm and excitement." How has God been evident in your life? Tell that story. What are your own gifts and talents…utilize these…share these gifts…and talents when you share the Good News?

Learning-to-action exercise

1. In your own words, how do you define evangelism in sports ministry?

____

____

____

2. Let's assume you, as a college student, wanted to start a sports ministry at your college or university based on your favorite sport, what are some of the first things that you would do, from an evangelism perspective to encourage people to join?

Sport(s)?:_____________________________________

Based on your expanded understanding of evangelism now, list some evangelism efforts below:

a.____

____

____

b.____

____

____

c.____

____

____

CHAPTER FOUR

LEADERSHIP

and Leadership Development in Sports Ministry

Chris Phillips
Recreation Minister and Equip Pastor
Bellevue Baptist Church, Memphis, TN
@chrisut
CSRM Board of Trustee Member

I began my service in ministry through local church sports and held lay leadership positions that aided in my growth as a believer and leader.

The Church in which I currently serve, Bellevue Baptist Church, is over one hundred years old and the recreation ministry has been a part of the church for over 40 years. Our ministry oversees adult sports, youth sports, recreational activities, and fitness ministries for over 7,500 people per year, as well as supporting the other ministries in the church (e.g., Children's Ministry, Youth Ministry, and Adult Educational Ministry). In this chapter, I want to give a general overview of leadership in sports ministry, both ***lay leadership*** and staff led, as well as give practical advice on how to begin developing leaders in your current sports ministry context, no matter how big or small it is. If sports ministry is one of the open doors to the Gospel and the local church, then it is of vital importance that the right leadership is in place and developed to introduce the unchurched to the Gospel.

A **lay leader** is a member of the clergy in any congregation who has been chosen as a leader. Since lay leadership is not an ordained position, responsibilities vary according to the particular tradition to which he or she belongs, in this case, sports ministry.

Leadership development is an ongoing process that some argue never stops. The greatest impact for developing leaders is when training is customized around specific needs, such as sports ministry.

One of the reasons ***leadership development*** is of critical importance is because it is clearly laid out in Scripture as the model for unity in faith. Before engaging with leadership development from a biblical and structural standpoint, one must have a clear understanding the very foundation of leadership from a definitional and biblical perspective. Leadership is the ability to influence, encourage, and direct followers in their God-given call towards a God-given vision. God gave Paul the model and priority for Leadership Development. The Scripture reveals, "And he gave the apostles, the prophets, the evangelists, the shepherds and teachers, to equip the saints for the work of ministry, for building up the body of Christ, until we all attain to the unity of the faith and of the knowledge of the Son of God, to mature manhood, to the measure of the stature of the fullness of Christ…" (Ephesians 4:11-13) This model says that as ministry leaders, our role is to equip and develop other leaders so that ministry can take place. This passage also shows that complete unity and building up of the body of Christ is done through equipping the saints for ministry. Literally, as ministry leaders develop other leaders, we see maturity and unity taking place.

Leadership from a managerial perspective is described as a "process whereby an individual influences a group of individuals to achieve a common goal" (Northouse, 2015, p. 2.)

As you think back to opportunities you have had over the years in ***leadership***, I am sure you can recall times when you were developed and given chances to lead at a higher level than you previously held. Whether you succeeded right away or failed your way through an experience, that opportunity brought maturity in you that will last a lifetime. We can see in the Ephesian's passage quote above that ministry actually brings maturity and not vice-versa. Too often in ministry, we feel that we cannot ***empower*** leaders until they have reached maturity, but that is an unbiblical approach. As leaders, we are to develop saints and workers for ministry by giving them opportunities to lead, which may or may not bring success immediately.

Although leadership plays out in nearly every area of the Church, I fully believe there is no better place to develop leaders than on the ball fields and courts. Coach, leader, and captain are all terms synonymous with sports. Coaching, in one of its most basic forms is giving training or instruction to someone. Times are rare when the "captain" or "leader" of the team is not recognized for a performance (whether positive or negative), a play, or a discussion about where the team is headed. Captains are chosen most times by teammates because of leadership and influence on the team. "True leadership cannot be awarded, appointed, or assigned. It comes only from influence, and that cannot be mandated. It must be earned. The only thing a title can buy is a little time-either to increase your level of influence with others or to undermine it (Maxwell, 2007, p. 13). These terms are not exclusive to sports, but useful for the general leadership development process also. As people serve and lead in ministry, they need mentors to invest into their development, as well as having people they too are investing in. This model is clearly laid out in Scripture through the relationship with Paul and Timothy and the intention of replicating that into the lives of others as stated in 2 Timothy 2:2. Leadership, in its most basic form, is influence. Whether one is a leader, coach, captain, or manager, they are influencing one way or the other, for good or for bad.

One of the hardest areas to manage in sports and recreation ministry is placing competent, quality, skilled, and ministry-minded people on the fields or courts to coach a team. I will not go into great detail here as Chapter 6 of this handbook does this eloquently. The expectation for one coach is to be skilled in a sport, ministry minded, relationally oriented, organized and punctual, and then to use all of those skills while facilitating a practice or game. The fact of the matter is that the expectations for the coach of a youth sports team are standards that most ministers probably could not uphold themselves. Depending on how coaches are found for a particular ministry and policies that are in place, there may also be stipulations for church membership, small group involvement, etc. that play into who is on the field or court in the coveted "coach" position.

A **Life Group** is a small group of people from all different backgrounds that often get together for fellowship, discuss their faith journey, grow as a believer, learn about the Word of God, and serve those in need.

In the current ministry context where I serve, our first step is to find church members that are involved in ***life groups*** more than fifty-percent of the time. After a league registration, our starting point in filling coaching positions is looking for parents that meet those requirements. Prior to owning a process of developing leaders, our initial recruitment went something like this: "Hello Mr. Smith, I see that your son is playing baseball again this year, would you be interested in coaching his team?" Now, when priorities and policies are in place to select leaders that are church members, involved in small groups, and competent in certain areas, we are limited to the available options for who can coach. If our leagues are comprised of fifty to sixty percent non-church members, then we have already cut our pool of eligible coaches by more than half. If we are then only engaging those that are in small groups with a certain percentage of attendance, we are then cutting our pool of leaders again.

After the conversation unfolds with the aforementioned parent, we typically find out that Mr. Smith is extremely busy this season with work and other commitments and is therefore unable to assist us in coaching. When you have a ministry that is not focused on developing leaders, they will respond something like this: "Thanks Mr. Smith, I appreciate your willingness and maybe you'll have time with the next sport or next season for your son. I hope you enjoy the league this year." At the very moment we respond in this nature, we have just cut off all opportunities for someone to be developed as a leader. We have also just exhibited that we put a higher priority on leadership placement than we do on leadership development. Our focus in this example would be to have all responsibility and pressure on one position alone, the coach, and we show that there are no other opportunities to lead. This creates a problem within the ministry that trickles down into every other league, service opportunity, and hinders development of the ministry. This clearly reveals a leadership development issue.

I truly believe that our problems in sports ministry, and church in general, is not a lack of leadership or a lack of volunteers to help us further the work of the Kingdom of God. I believe the issue lies in the fact that we have not adhered to the Ephesians 4 passage about equipping saints for the work of ministry. I believe that we have not taken the time and effort to develop leaders and guide them in a direction of growing in their walk and service opportunities for the Lord. Todd Adkins, Leadership Director at Lifeway, says it best, "It's not a leadership problem as much as it is a leadership development problem" (Rainer, 2013). When only focusing on placing leaders in positions within the ministry and not developing them on a leadership pipeline, we are showing little value for other service opportunities within the ministry. As noted previously, our coaches in sports ministry cannot maintain the expectations we typically project on them, leading to inadequate ministry opportunities to reach those we have participating in our leagues. When placing leaders over developing them, we not only reveal leadership development issues, but also that our ministry is not running as effectively as it could be when there is emphasis on training and developing leaders.

Here are three strategies to help effectively engage those in your sports ministry:

1. **Affinity**: We all need to believe in something. Help people believe in what they do whether it's coaching or answering phones.

If we use the same example as mentioned above, but have a focus on developing leaders, the outcome looks drastically different. In our current ministry mindset, we are not focusing solely on the coach of the team, but the support group of leaders around the coach. Using the same baseball example, we want to identify leaders that can support the coach in ministry efforts. In order to fully minister to those in the league, we have identified that we will need some of the following leadership positions: assistant coach, team shepherd, prayer leader, and team leader (team mom). These positions will aid the coach in teaching the skill, reaching out to the families involved, praying for the team and identifying prayer needs, as well as setting up snacks, sending out reminders, and organizing team functions or parties.

2. **Affiliation**: People want to belong to something. Make an effort for those involved in your sports ministry to be involved.

3. **Autonomy**: Give your coaches the ability to find and deliver their own message. You help here will likely be needed, but having people develop their own message will make all three of these "As" that much stronger.

By successfully taking these burdens off the coach, we are not only allowing a greater focus on teaching skill, but also allowing a greater ministry opportunity by giving time to engage with players, parents, and family that shows up for games and practices. This allows for relational evangelism and opportunities to encourage and strengthen those in the Word of God. This process also allows the ministry to build and develop a plethora of leaders that can effectively engage and support the ministry, no matter the number of participants that register.

Moving alongside of the same example used above, our conversation changes dramatically when we are engaging leaders to serve in the ministry. The conversation now looks something like this: "Hello Mr. Smith, I see that your son is playing baseball again this year, would you be interested in coaching his team?" After you find out that Mr. Smith cannot serve as a coach this year, our question can then be directed like this: "I can definitely understand the busy-ness and how hard that is to manage Mr. Smith. I'd like to talk with you about another couple of options that might not take as much commitment as a coach, but are vital to us ministering to the teams we have this year. Do you think you would have time to be a prayer leader, assistant coach, or a team shepherd? These would not require the same commitment, but you would be engaging in relationships on the team that would further the gospel and honestly, be more important than coaching a sports skill…" No matter how busy Mr. Smith is, the least that he could do is be a prayer leader for the team, which would not even require him to be at games and practices.

Now, fully trusting the work of the Lord in Mr. Smith's life, I know, believe, and have personally seen people be engaged in something as easy as praying and it turn into larger leadership positions within the ministry. As Mr. Smith is developed as a leader, shown the importance of the work in the sports ministry, and continued to be invested in, next season, next year, or next child, Mr. Smith will be more than willing to aid in coaching because he has been taken down a path of development and not merely placed into a position. This pipeline of leaders that are being developed is not something new to ministry or churches, but has been used in the business world for quite some time. Businesses frequently discuss the importance of training up the next generation of leaders within an organization, but similar to ministry, also discuss a shortage of leaders. They too are susceptible to leadership placement rather than leadership development. This development of leaders on the stages of a pipeline allows organizations and ministries to evaluate and develop a pool of leaders to take them to another level of leading. Ram Charan, author of *The Leadership Pipeline* explains, "Instead of vague determinations that a company is lacking a talent pool of young leaders, the pipeline approach enables you to locate the exact level where problems are occurring and the skills, time applications, and values at that level where people are coming up short" (Charan, Drotter & Noel, 2010, p. 164). There is not a shortage of leaders in your sports ministry, but there is more than likely a shortage of development in a pipeline of leaders that is causing problems with filling positions of need.

Although this process might seem overwhelming at first, there are some practical steps to take when beginning this process in your current ministry context that are vital pieces of information that must be looked at in order to successfully begin developing leaders.

1. **Evaluate your current system and structure.**
2. **Define the layers of leaders you have or wish to have.**
3. **Define leader descriptions and proficiencies.**

Evaluate your current system and structure

There is an old leadership adage that you cannot expect what you do not inspect. In order for you to completely begin a leadership development process, you must be able to fully communicate and understand the current structure and process you have in place. In the world of sports ministry, one can easily get bogged down with running the programs and everything that entails, which removes one's ability to think logically about the ***systems and structures*** that are in place. When the answer to "why" we are doing something is "because we've always done it that way," then this is a key indicator that change needs to happen.

Systems and structures specify the relationships between the people that perform tasks and the tasks themselves.

Evaluating the structure of a sports ministry program is a very

Sports ministry managers should be evaluating their programs on a regular basis. Evaluation consists of measuring and ensuring progress toward program objectives are met.

Evaluation can occur in several stages such as:

1. After an event
2. After a season
3. At the end of the year.

Best practices would incorporate all three of the above. Research by Dr. Smith (2016) found that the evaluation process of sport ministers is often overlooked due to the time constraints involved. Please see Appendix A for examples of evaluation forms.

healthy process for every ministry to go through. Look at your current training, leadership covenants, expectations, forms, recruitment, etc. Write out this entire process and look at it with your staff, lay teams, committees, or whomever it is that you run approvals through in your ministry. Another best practice with ***evaluating*** is to compare your system and structure to other ministries within the church. Ask them for their system and compare what it would look like for a first time guest in sports ministry compared to worship service, adult education, youth ministry, etc. This process will not only help you evaluate your current development process, but also enable you to have similar language to your counterparts in other ministry segments to provide familiarity for leaders.

When performing an evaluation, it is also vital to look at the leadership job description. Do you have a document in place with expectations and proficiencies you desire your leaders to have? We will talk about this more in third point, but the evaluation will reveal whether or not you have set clear expectations. "Without a good diagnostic tool we often mistake output for leadership effectiveness" (Charan, Drotter & Noel, 2010, p. 165). There are many benefits to an evaluation of your current system. Doing one will:

1. Allow your people to have clear expectations for what is desired. With an evaluation, clear examples and job descriptions are required, thus giving your follower an opportunity to look at roles, responsibilities, and even time frames involved in the leadership position.

2. Create simplicity for development. With an evaluation, the leader knows the exact areas of improvement for the follower, as they are moving along your leadership pipeline.

3. Create a route for development. With an evaluation, the leader and follower know exactly where they stand on a leadership pipeline and thus understand what it will take to move to another level of leadership.

4. Give an opportunity to analyze where you are currently having issues. When an evaluation is captured, leadership holes will be identified and the leadership team can begin working on filling those holes with followers from the organization.

5. Help you align with other ministries within the church. With an evaluation and common language, ministries will remove the silo mentality and can more easily work with each other to fill gaps and holes in their leadership pipeline.

Although the evaluation takes time, effort, and energy, it is an extremely beneficial practice for your ministry and ministry team.

Define the layers of leaders you have or wish to have

Leadership development is not an overnight method, but a process that will take time, effort, and consistency. When defining your current and future layers of leaders, you must think and understand that it will take time for you to have all of the leaders that are needed or desired. Defining your layers of leaders is a road map of what you desire your ministry to look like. If you want to have a coach, assistant coach, team mom, and prayer leader for youth baseball, then you must define these positions and what their leadership responsibilities include. When defining your layers of leaders, you must indicate what you would desire to have on every team that comes through your ministry. One sport may look different than the next, but you must define each leader and what his or her roles include.

The process of defining your leaders will provide clarity for what each league, team, or activity needs in terms of leadership. This leadership list will also allow you to identify areas where you are weak or strong in terms of leadership, and it will assist you in your recruitment efforts. If you have 40 leadership positions, but you only have 15 filled, then you will be able to effectively recruit for the remaining 25 leadership positions, knowing that some may be for an assistant, while others may be a prayer leader or team mom. Too often, when one does not have a defined list with their layers of leadership, they are more prone to place leaders in certain areas where they are not equipped or ready to serve. These layers and needs will change depending on the number of teams in the league, but a good starting point is to define the number of teams with the number of leaders you have and not vice-versa. When using the number of teams to identify leaders needed, a ministry is more prone to placement of leaders as opposed to development, and quality begins to take a hit. When you provide quality over quantity, quantity can always rise, but the same is not the case for when quantity is the first focus.

Define leadership descriptions and proficiencies.

Job descriptions are critical for any position within your sports ministry program, including and especially for volunteers. "A job description is a written statement of what a job holder does, how it is done and why it is done. The description typically describes job content, environment, and conditions of the position" (Robbins, Coulter & Langton, 2006, p. 305). Please see Appendix B of this chapter for an example of a job description.

Once the leadership positions have been properly identified, the ministry must begin to discern exactly what the ***job descriptions*** and proficiencies are for each leader. Ministries must begin to ask, what exactly do I need the coach of the youth baseball team to do? Far too often, when programs begin and the hustle of getting committed leaders steals most of one's time, the quality and clarity of what our leaders are expected to do falls to the bottom of the list. When this happens, placement of leaders becomes the focus, and development of them according to their defined descriptions and proficiencies is no longer a factor. If a ministry does not clearly define the description of the leadership position, then their success becomes extremely hard to identify. As we noted, we cannot inspect what we do not expect from our leaders and if there are no clear expectations set through descriptions and proficiencies desired, then it becomes tough to develop people on their journey. Keep in mind; if we aim for nothing, then we will hit it every time.

Proficiencies for each leadership position will not only help one identify success for the leader, but it will also give a starting point for leaders at lower levels to aim for growth so they can eventually lead at a higher level within the ministry. For example, if the prayer leader knows that a proficiency of the assistant coach is to develop relationships with members of the team, then when they feel the urge to move up as leaders, they can focus on how they will develop relationships with team members and become proficient enough to lead at a higher level.

The proficiencies are referred to in some leadership circles as competencies (Adkins, n. d.). These competencies then become the baseline for how one develops their leaders. Training that leads to competency is mastery, not knowledge transfer (Adkins, n. d.). When leaders become proficient and competent in their leadership ability, they can be described as having proper knowledge, coaching, and experience, which combined gives them the ability to lead at a high level. When training a coach with knowledge transfer via forms, articles, or books, it does not lead to a properly developed leader, but just a person with merely information on how to be one. When training a coach with only coaching and instruction for skill, it does not provide the necessary information needed to understand the position. Finally, training a coach with only experience just gives a learn as you go mentality and hinders leadership as well. All of these areas separately obstruct the overall leadership development process, but when combined together produces a leader who is proficient and ready to lead at any level.

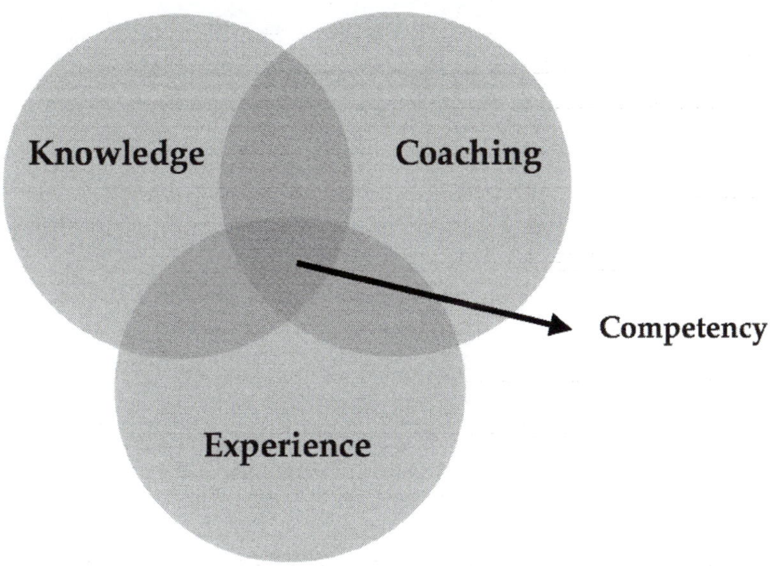

Figure 1. Competency Venn Diagram

There is no way ministry, in any context, can be successfully sustained with a lack of leaders. As noted, the church and ministries therein are not void of leaders, but void of a development process to put leaders in place. The "Jethro Principle" is a common biblical reference to the need for developing leaders for the work of ministry. Sports ministry can be exhausting, both physically and emotionally, and the burden cannot solely remain on the staff. As referred to in the "Jethro Principle," leaders must take on the responsibility of developing others to help them do the work required to run ministry. For your sports ministry, an evaluation is necessary, structures must be defined, and proficiencies and descriptions listed, and leaders must be developed to produce a quality product on the fields and courts for believers and non-believers to enjoy. When leaders are properly developed, they are freed to hone in on doing the work of ministry and sharing the Gospel of Christ to bring lost souls from death to life, as well as aiding in the sanctification process of believers.

Learning-to-action exercise

1. After reading this chapter, list three (3) areas in which you can become a better leader.

a. ______________________________

b. ______________________________

c. ______________________________

2. List three (3) people that you know that you think you could work with to become better leaders and how could you help them become a better leader.

Person A ______________________________

How: ______________________________

____

Person B ______________________________

How: ______________________________

____

Person C ______________________________

How: ______________________________

____

3. What are three (3) leadership development areas that you can work on TODAY and why?

a. ______________________________

Why? ______________________________

b. ______________________________

Why? ______________________________

c. ______________________________

Why? ______________________________

Appendix A

Leadership Pipeline Overview
Youth Sports

RECREATION Ministry

Pipeline Level	Leadership Responsibility	Core Competencies: Discipleship	Core Competencies: Vision	Core Competencies: Strategy	Core Competencies: Collaboration	Core Competencies: People Development	Core Competencies: Stewardship	Ministry-Specific Compenticies
Progression	Descriptions	Theological and Spritual Development	Preferred Future	Plan or Method for the Preferred Future	Ability to Work with Others	Contributing to the Growth of Others	Overseeing Resources Within One's Care	Unique Skills Within Ministry Area

Bellevue

Adult Ministry - Life Groups Training Audit

Training Resources	Description	Prayer Partner	Assistant Coach	Youth Sports Coach	Divisional Leader	Youth Sports Commissioner	Youth Sports Director/Minister
Confidential Volunteer Application	Does this position fill one out?						
Job Description	Is there a job description for this position?						
Time Commitment	What is the time frame expectation for this position? (i.e. 1 year, 2 years, continual, etc.)						
Orientation Training	Is there a standardized process to train new leaders in this position?						
Ongoing Training	Is there structured process to continually train leaders? (i.e. online, continuing education, etc.)						
Evaluation	Is there a structured evaluation process for this position that is disccused with the leader?						
Inspiration	Do you have a "leader/volunteer appreciation" for your leadership positions as a time of encouragement?						

Bellevue

Leadership Pipeline Overview

____________ Ministry

Pipeline Level	Leadership Responsibility	Roles	Number of Roles	Number of Leaders	
Progression	Descriptions	Examples	Current	Current	Desired
This Person… **Leads Church**	Provides visionary leadership for church as a whole				
This Person… **Leads Ministries**	Provides visionary leadership to multiple ministries				
This Person… **Leads Departments**	Oversees a ministry with responsibility of leading leaders				
This Person… **Leads Leaders**	Leads a group of leaders within a specific ministry				
This Person… **Leads Others**	Provides leadership for a small group of people				
This Person… **Leads Self**	Serves on a Ministry Team				

RECREATION Ministry

Leadership Pipeline Overview
Youth Sports

Pipeline Level	Leadership Responsibility	Core Competencies						
		Discipleship	Vision	Strategy	Collaboration	People Development	Stewardship	Ministry-Specific Compenticies
Progression	Descriptions	Theological and Spritual Development	Preferred Future	Plan or Method for the Preferred Future	Ability to Work with Others	Contributing to the Growth of Others	Overseeing Resources Within One's Care	Unique Skills Within Ministry Area
Youth Sports Commissioner								Specific competencies will vary depening on the role and the specific ministry area the leader is serving. The competencies are the areas that the leaders will grow and you will be able to check off whether they are growing in the specific areas laid out per ministry role. These competencies will aid in your future leadership development of each role.
League Administrator								
Divisional Leader								
Team Shepherd / Connector								
Coach								
Asst. Coach								
Prayer Leader	Praying by name over league participants	Knows the power of prayer and ability for God to move via prayer	Articulates vision for the prayer ministry	Leads others to unite around praying for our players and league	Works with and through others and builds relationships	Disiplays initiative to develop and enlists prayer warriors	Faithfully stewards gifteedness, time, and invests in others	* Scripturally knowledgeable on prayer. * Dedicated to undivided prayer time
Volunteer	Serves on a Ministry Team	Knows the Gospel and takes personal responsibility for Development	Supports Vision of the Ministry Area they're serving	Serve effectively in desired area	Works with others	Displays initiative to be developed	Faithfully stewards giftedness and time	* Flexibility with Time * Willingness to serve * Spiritual Awares of serving

Appendix B

SERVE IN JOB DESCRIPTION
EXAMPLE

TITLE: Volunteer Head Coach – Recreation

JOB SUMMARY: Lead a group of youth participants to learn skills of a specific sport while also gaining knowledge of sportsmanship, servant-leadership, and Biblical Truth. Encourage the youth to learn how to play sports in a gospel-centered manner.

COMPETENCIES:
1. Has knowledge of the game and understands the rules specific to the sport they are coaching.
2. Able to communicate effectively to both children and adults.
3. Capable of leading a practice for a given sport in a Christ-honoring way.
4. Is able to motivate, encourage, and lead in a Christ-honoring way.
5. Can handle confrontation within and outside a game setting.
6. Has physical ability to demonstrate specific skills of the sport.

TIME COMMITMENT:

Weeknight –
1 Hour of the following: (Mon./Tues./Thurs.)
6:00pm; 7:00pm; 8:00pm

Saturday – 1 Hour of the following:
9:00am; 10:00am; 11:00am; 12:00pm; 1:00pm

LENGTH OF SERVICE:
8-10 weeks, depending on the sport

WORKING RELATIONSHIP: Recreation Staff team

TRAINING: Attend a pre-season coaches meeting. Complete our Confidential Volunteer Application. View given resources (blogs, books, and videos) from Recreation staff and participate in continued on-the-job training.

MINISTRY CONTACTS: Youth Sports Minister and Minister of Recreation

CHAPTER FIVE

COUNTERACTING
a Lone Ranger Leadership Mentality

Tinsley Jones
Director of Recreation Ministry
Crestwood Presbyterian Church
Richmond, VA

Unlike my current situation as the sole sports ministry manager, other sports ministries have dedicated staff positions to oversee and direct the ministry efforts; others are led by volunteer roles.

Whether a ministry has a multi-person staff, a solo staff person, or no dedicated staff person at all does not determine if a ministry is effective or not. We have to remember that sports outreach ministries will not all look the same, yet, we can certainly learn from one another, no matter how similar we feel. I have been through some challenging times, many of these challenges have become very rewarding experiences, but I wanted to write this chapter from my perspective as the lone sports ministry manager, a manager and staff of one, a Lone Ranger.

A Lone Ranger perspective

Let me take a moment to explain my specific ministry context in regards to staffing. As the ministry's director and staff of one, all aspects of developing and maintaining the ministry are my responsibility, which means I have many hats to wear. Therefore, I keep a proverbial hat rack in my office in order to make quick changes. Some of the hats include budgeting, marketing, administration, recruitment, vision casting, registration, communication, and program implementation, to name a few. Each hat represents a different role to embody or task to be completed and at times, certain roles or tasks take priority over others. Please consider this disclaimer: managing all aspects of the ministry alone is not a healthy choice, especially regarding your longevity as a sport minister. We need to keep the broader picture in play here, knowing that sports ministry is an opportunity to deliver God's message, to be disciples to the Lord, doing a ministry alone is better than having no ministry at all. A ministry managed alone is challenging; maintaining focus and attending to all details related to directing a ministry without support and assistance from others, is ill advised. ***Burnout*** may occur as the individual leading and administering the ministry alone becomes tired, discouraged, and frustrated. Without support, input, and value found from other ministry advocates, the enthusiasm of the sport minister may become dim.

Burnout is a common occurrence in the workplace. Additional job burnout psychological characteristics are: exhaustion, lack of enthusiasm, motivation and feelings of ineffectiveness. (Jackson, Schwab & Schuler, 1986)

It may sound a bit bleak that a sports ministry may struggle to survive with only one staff person managing and overseeing the entire ministry; however, a staff of one can certainly be effective, I must be doing something right, I have been doing it for five years now! Support is needed, however, support is not always there at the time you need it, and recruiting volunteers for assistance will be important. Managing a ministry on your own can be done, of course, and done extremely well. This chapter is not intended to discourage managing a ministry with a staff of one; rather, the intentions of this chapter is to give a perspective of how to best manage the ministry on your own, because at some point as a sports minister, this will occur…all decisions, the direction, and the methods of the ministry come from one person. In this chapter, that one person is termed a Lone Ranger leader. But the essence of this chapter is to identify the Lone Ranger mentality and attempt to break that mold.

Being a Lone Ranger sport minister may appear to have its advantages. Without input from others one may feel decisions can be made on a faster timeline, with less bureaucracy slowing down the decision-making or implementation process. Another perceived advantage might be that only one person is needed to carry out the vision of the ministry. Lone Ranger sport ministers may feel and often fall into the mentality that no other input is needed or even wanted from anyone else. On the contrary, most of those perceived advantages are centered on clenching onto and maintaining control of the ministry form and direction; or perhaps, they are stimulated by a belief that others are not needed in order to effectively spur ministry efforts or that others simply do not care or value the ministry. In contrast to those perceived advantages, a Lone Ranger leadership style may begin to form and actually stifle growth and development. Trying to juggle all tasks and complete all details solo is a recipe for burnout as well and is, quite simply, a reckless approach to leading your sports ministry in a positive direction. I have been down this road of a Lone Ranger leadership mentality. I thought I could do it, but in the long run, it hindered my performance and hindered the ministry.

Neutralize the Lone Ranger mentality

Sports and recreation outreach ministries come in many different shapes and sizes. Variables include facility space, budget allowance, congregation size, staff resources, and more. These variables do not define the potential of ministry efforts; however, they are certainly context specific. What works for one sports ministry may or may not work for another ministry based on many of the variables mentioned. Understanding your ministries specific context, rather than comparing or sizing up one context over another, can aid in efficiently managing a sports outreach ministry, especially when you are starting a ministry on your own, or have been managing a ministry by yourself for years...like I have.

Whether you are starting a sports ministry or are a part of an existing ministry, how does one determine their specific ministry context? Identifying the context of a sports and recreation ministry involves multiple ***stakeholders*** and available resources that include the active members in the church, the strengths and needs of the congregation, the strength and needs of the community, and the facilities and resources available to the ministry. Additional factors that make up a ministry context include the overall church mission and vision for conducting a sports and recreation ministry. The broad goal of any sports and recreation ministry leader is to identify and maintain an active reading of the pulse of the context in which it functions.

Stakeholders are those individuals that have a direct interest or concern with the success of the sport ministry both internal of the ministry *(e.g., senior pastor)* or external of the ministry. *(e.g., local business owner).*

A practical step in gauging and evaluating context is to consider what is currently being done in your own recreation and sports ministry. This will help break that mold of a Lone Ranger mentality as you are actively seeking input about other programs in your area that may have been designed or implemented by another ministry in a different context. For example, certain communities may have particular affinities towards specific sports or activities. Basketball is a popular sport in Indiana whereas soccer or football may be more popular on the East Coast. This does not suggest a soccer ministry cannot be produced in Indiana; however, understanding the community that surrounds your church is a step in identifying the context in which you are serving. Not all ministry initiatives are cookie-cutter, one-size-fits all type endeavors. Learning from the practices of other ministries is extremely beneficial; yet, doing so from a lens of one's own specific context will prove more advantageous in the end. Before planning a new ministry initiative or reinventing an existing one, the strategy and planning involved will be informed by context elements noted above, not vice versa.

So, what, then, can be done to counteract a Lone Ranger leadership mentality when you work as a staff of one? First and foremost, know that it will likely happen to those that work alone, but also know that once identified, it can be quickly adjusted. I think a few foundational steps can be implemented to widen the nets to bring others alongside to be involved in the ministry efforts. My hope is that my experiences within these steps will inspire you to evaluate your own leadership style and make changes when needed. Below, I've highlighted five steps that I believe are instrumental in counteracting the pull to lead and manage alone.

1. Cast mission & vision

And Jesus said to them, ***"Follow me, and I will make you become fishers of men."*** (Mark 1:17)

As my colleagues have noted within this book, it is important to understand the mission and vision of your broader organization, whether it being a church or other faith community. In order to effectively lead others within a sports ministry (e.g., volunteers), the leader knowing and communicating the direction and purpose of the ministry is utterly important. Without a mission or purpose for the ministry, the path and way to carry out the ministry efforts really does not matter because no course has been set; however, with a mission in mind, staying the course to accomplish the ministry's purposes certainly does matter. So know the church mission, understand the mission and how it applies to your sports ministry. Casting vision illuminates the path to others involved within the ministry in order for the mission to be accomplished. A ministry leader must continually and effectively communicate a clear vision to those involved within the ministry. Yes, this will require up-front effort on the part of the ministry leader to develop a concise and concrete mission and vision for the ministry, and one that supports and fits with the broader mission of the church with which the ministry is a part. Such work will bear fruit as others become involved and understand the purpose and reasons to support the ministry efforts. A sound, clear vision can be contagious and will attract and spark the interest of others to become involved. See the specific mission and vision of Crestwood Presbyterian Church Recreation Ministry in the appendix of Chapter 6

Whether or not you find yourself in a staff of one, be sure to take the initiative to connect with other sports ministry practitioners in your local area. Being connected to like-minded individuals in the field will broaden your understanding and benefit your personal growth and development. Coordinating a monthly meeting with other sports ministry directors to exchange ideas and offer support for one another can be motivational as a sole sport minister. I have done it, and it has proven beneficial for me personally, professionally, and spiritually.

2. Build a leadership team

Even so the body is not made up of one part but of many. (1 Corinthians 12:14)

To counter a Lone Ranger leadership mentality, a solid foundation must be laid within any context of a local church's recreation and sports ministry. This foundation includes building a leadership team to invest in the recreation and sports ministry of the church. From a practical standpoint, building a leadership team helps carry the load of leading a vibrant sports ministry. A team united around the mission and vision of the ministry brings an array of insight, talents, and voices speaking into the direction and form of the ministry. Without a leadership team, a Lone Ranger leader will be making decisions without the invested input of others and a broader perspective will also be lacking without a team in place. A leadership team provides balance and accountability, specifically in a ministry setting where the ministry is led by a staff of one. I was not always blessed to have a consistent team when working with volunteers, but possibilities are out there especially when developing relationships with high schools or college and university Physical Education or Sport Management departments.

For ministry to flourish, we need people. Going it alone is hasty, even reckless. Ministry leader's need to connect with others in the mission and vision of ministry. Otherwise, creativity is suppressed and ministry potential squandered. Utilizing resources such as The Association of Church Sports and Recreation Ministries (csrm.org), the North American Society of Sport Management (nassm.com) or Cede Sports (cedesports.org) or attending conferences like the REACHGathering or the Christian Society for Kinesiology, Leisure, and Sports Studies (cskls.org) Annual conference are great ways to build your network.

No matter the context, gifted individuals are present in a congregation. God has gifted individuals uniquely and beautifully. The gifts

[5] You can simply Google any one of these association names or conferences to learn more of what they have to offer and they will most certainly build your network.

and talents of others blended and poured into a ministry's efforts will provide a fuller, richer picture of what and how God intends for the ministry to realize its vision and purpose. A team of people represents the communal nature of God that a single leader cannot do alone. Recruiting and building a leadership team is paramount to counteracting the Lone Ranger leadership mentality. You need to seek it out, you need to articulate the mission and vision, and recruiting begins with your own congregation. Remember, individuals will follow a compelling vision. For a vision to be compelling it must evoke the attention and interest of others in a powerful, irresistible way. Knowing what type of leadership team to which you are recruiting is also important. Is this an administrative or logistics team, or rather, is this a team charged with setting and guiding the direction of the sports outreach ministry? Those two teams will clearly have different purposes, and so it is important for the leader to be clear in the function of the team. Both types are needed, yet for both to be more effective, those two types of teams need not be lumped into one team. Simply, because then the purpose of the team will be muddled; thus, its effectiveness to carry out its purpose will be compromised as well. In order to recruit team members, the leader must also be able to identify the qualities desired of the team members that will join the leadership team. As aforementioned, a team represents an array of gifts and talents. Having a variety of skills represented will prove advantageous. As the sports ministry leader communicates the vision and purpose for the leadership team, God will bring members to the team. I encourage you to use the characteristics discussed in this step in addition to Bob Schindler discussion of recruiting, training, and retaining coaches to assist you in building your leadership team. You can find this information in the very next chapter.

3. Share stories

Great is the Lord and most worthy of praise; his greatness no one can fathom. One generation commends your works to another; they tell of your mighty acts. (Psalm 145:3-4)

Sharing stories is a critical piece in the building of a sports ministry program. People want to know what you are doing, especially those that may be skeptical. Have several stories to share, but keep them brief and to the point. Those that want to know more about the story or ministry will ask, but you do not want to become frustrated with telling stories that go on and on.

Story example #1

Our Recreation Ministry has administered a spring volleyball league for middle school-aged participants the past few years. The league was started from scratch after a series of volleyball clinics we ran one fall season. Even though some risk was involved in launching a new league, we felt we could build from the momentum and interest in the clinics the season prior to the initial launch of the league. Yet, we really did not know if we would have enough interest that first season to even conduct a league. Despite the initial risk, our volleyball initiative has proven to be a positive one for our ministry in a number of ways. It continues to grow each year due primarily to ***word-of-mouth*** communication from participants and parents to others in the community. Such organic growth communicates to us that parents and families are enjoying a positive experience. We often hear parents of the participants share enthusiasm and delight in watching their young teenager be introduced to a new sport. Some of the participants in our league have yet to find their "sport" or have never participated on a team of any kind. It truly is a joy to watch them blossom over the course of the season. Not only do their volleyball skills develop, but their confidence and social awareness do as well. Our hope is that our ministry provides an affirming atmosphere, where participants learn biblical truth that can be applied to their real-life experiences. For example, one truth to be gained is that players have value on the team, no matter their role, position, or ability. Additionally, we hope our league leaders, coaches, administrators, etc., are living congruently to what they are communicating and teaching each week of the season.

Word-of-mouth is the best form of marketing and advertising for any organization. Maximizing this technique is critical for growth of your sports ministry.

Story example #2

I remember one family sharing that their daughter was extremely nervous about joining a league where she may not know anyone and playing a sport she had never attempted. Her parents said they knew her to be shy and cautious of new experiences. She said to her parents, "What if I'm not good enough to play? What if the other players think I'm hurting the team? What if no one likes me because I don't play volleyball well?" She continued to wonder what it would be like and after her parents encouraged her, she did eventually decide to participate. Over the course of the season, she began to learn the basics about volleyball. Although some participants had previously played and had some familiarity with the sport, she realized she was not the only player with limited experience. Her coaches were extremely patient and encouraging. They did not show favoritism, and they taught the skills in ways she could understand and made the practices fun. She began to make friends and could tell the team was beginning to gel. One skill she had difficulty mastering was serving. Although she felt embarrassed at times, her teammates always encouraged her. Her coaches had taught the team that no matter what, they are a team, and they must encourage and support one another. Her parents were floored as they witnessed their daughter gain more confidence. They were not concerned with how well she served, rather they were more encouraged by her demeanor on the court and the joy they saw her exhibiting. I have to say, as a recreation ministry director, of course, I enjoy watching our participants thrive. However, over the years, I have realized just how heartwarming it is to observe the parents' delight in watching their own children begin to prosper and develop and find joy in our ministry efforts. Plus, not only did their daughter enjoy her experience in our volleyball league, she returned for another season, and she has communicated to our leadership that she wants to return as a volunteer in some capacity once she ages out of the league. She entered into the league with much trepidation, yet she took a risk and found a sport and means to build confidence, athletically and socially. She grew spiritually as she realized that every player on the team is created by God and has intrinsic value. Thus, everyone brings something unique to the team, including her.

That is one story we share about our ministry when people ask what really goes on between the walls of the gymnasium. We want members of our congregation and our community to know that our ministry is not just about fun and games (although we do want their experience to be a positive and joyful one). I once heard a sports ministry practitioner refer to stories shared within their specific ministry as "impact stories." That term immediately resonated with me and has stuck with me ever since because people can relate to stories; they respond to them; they are impacted by them. People will remember a story more vividly than a bullet list of dry facts and statistics, not matter how accurate and factual those details are. A story can communicate the impact a ministry is having, and likewise, the story impacts those who hear it. An impact story can, in a way, be a tool for casting vision, too. Sharing stories is an excellent method to highlight the purpose of the ministry as well as its corresponding impact and can inspire others to become involved or support the ministry in some way. Be creative in the manner that the story is shared. Personal testimony from a participant of the ministry is always a strong option; yet, creating videos, posting on social media, and writing blogs or articles are also effective and viable ways to share stories. Know your audience and choose the medium accordingly. Make sharing impact stories a priority, as those stories will convey a common, shared experience and knowledge to a broader audience. Stories have a way of being remembered and then retold, what an impact, indeed.

4. Perform a SWOT analysis

Let us examine our ways and test them, and let us return to the Lord. (Lamentations 3:40)

Self-awareness includes identifying your strengths as well as your weaknesses and should occur on a regular basis.

To be an effective leader, one must be *self-aware*. Strengths can be accentuated, where weaknesses can be compensated through the gifts and talents of others involved in the ministry. Scott (2014) suggested that individuals and sport organizations must occasionally evaluate their own personal and organizational goals and desired outcomes to determine strategies for future possibilities. There is a business and management techniques called a SWOT analysis, often used to study organizations. The great asset to this technique is that individuals as well to become better at managing your ministry can also utilize it.

When performing an individual analysis, the S & W represent your Strengths and Weaknesses. Strengths and Weaknesses embody the internal efforts over which individuals are likely to have direct control. My personal strengths and weaknesses will, of course, be unique to me. For example, my strengths include administration, communication, and organization. These serve me well in managing a ministry and its corresponding programming. My weaknesses include difficulty in delegating leadership needs, specifically higher levels of leadership. I am more apt to delegate tasks related to administration or managing logistics and details, rather than ministry leadership. My areas for growth and improvement include identifying those that have leadership ability and then recruiting and developing them into a leader for a specific ministry aspect or program.

The O & W represent the Opportunities and Threats that embody the external characteristics over which an individual may not have direct control. However, from an external perspective, what opportunities are encountered and what threats to avoid, at times, may be influenced by the individual, or perhaps, in some cases, those threats can be turned into growth opportunities. Like my strengths and weaknesses, my opportunities and threats will be unique to me as well. For example, my opportunities include the chance to shape our ministry's direction and form to people outside of our existing sports ministry program. When I began at Crestwood, much opportunity existed to create more robust and diverse recreation ministry programming. When I arrived I was told I had freedom to be creative because the ministry form had yet to take its full shape. Similarly, though, a threat along those same lines in my personal ministry context would be others' resistance to change. As I continue to direct and shape the ministry, specific to making any changes, it is possible I could be met with discontent or resistance from others. To combat such friction, it would be helpful for our leadership team to be sure we are effectively communicating our ministry mission and vision on a consistent basis. Without a full picture on where the ministry is headed, some may feel uneasy about any changes. Here, the threat could be changed into an opportunity by sharing our purpose and plan for ministry with a larger audience. Being prepared and anticipating any possible threats can help avoid any additional pitfalls as well.

Personal SWOT analysis of Tinsley Jones:

	STRENGTHS	**WEAKNESSES**
Internal	Administration, Communication, Organized	Delegating and developing higher levels of leadership
	OPPORTUNITIES	**THREATS**
External	To shape the ministry's direction and form	Resistance to change from others

You will have a chance to perform your own personal SWOT analysis below

5. Step away from the Silo

Now you are the body of Christ, and each one of you is a part of it. (1 Corinthians 12:27)

In certain scenarios, a silo can serve a positive purpose. In agriculture, for example, a silo is a tall structure used to store grain and other materials in bulk. The purpose of a silo in the context of sports ministry is certainly a constructive one. However, within a management context, working in a silo, where collaboration and communication is nonexistent or minimal, at best, is not conducive to strong levels of productivity and efficiency. Unfortunately, some staff and ministry structures within the local church represent the silo approach, where ministries operate as stand-alone entities rather than partners in collaboration striving to accomplish a shared, unified mission.

In the context of the local church, a sports ministry may be more prone to operate as a silo. Sports ministries tend to have a different rhythm and cadence than other more traditional ministries of the local church. For example, running youth or adult sport leagues as part of the sports ministry can produce a different schedule (e.g., weeknight practices and weekend games) than other ministries within the church. Some key volunteers, such as coaches or officials, may hail from the surrounding community rather than from within the congregation. Having community members involved in the ministry has many advantages and need not be considered taboo, yet it can also inadvertently create or widen a schism between the sports outreach ministry and other ministries within the church that are predominately fueled by members of the congregation, simply because those in the congregation may not understand the sports ministry due to lack of involvement from those connected to the church. As such, many sports ministry leaders can feel misunderstood (perhaps because the mission and vision has yet to be defined and clearly communicated to others within the church). If a ministry leader feels misunderstood, or perhaps worse, de-valued, then the high walls of the silo may begin to rise and further isolate the ministry from other ministries of the church. Just because ministry looks different within a sports and recreation setting than it may look within other ministries of the church does not result in those ministry efforts being of little value to the larger mission of the church. Looking different is not a reason to isolate the ministry within a silo. Rather, looking different, whether in schedule or methods or rhythm, actually highlights the vast, viable ways ministry happens within the setting of the local church.

Particularly to those sports outreach ministries that are led by one staff member, one important nugget of advice must be shared. Step away from the silo. Do not enter in one. Instead, link up with others within the staff and congregation and find ways to support other staff members, volunteers, and ministries within the church. Remember, the ministries of the church need to be united in mission and purpose, not divided. How the mission is carried out may look different, yes, but not the mission itself. The sports outreach ministry supports and upholds the mission of the church. Even with different methods, ministries of the church can find joint synergy and ways to partner and work together. Seek out these opportunities. Be a team player, and tear down the high walls of the silo if you begin to recognize one is forming or experience operating within one.

These five steps do not represent an exhaustive list on how to counteract a Lone Ranger leadership mentality; however, they do represent a strong start. A major responsibility of a ministry leader is to equip others to operate and lead within the ministry as well. Relying on one's own abilities and not involving others is a distorted view of leadership. Even further, without reliance on our Creator God, to whom we strive to bring glory, a sports outreach ministry will never reach its full potential to impact others for the glory of God. For a sports ministry to flourish, a reliance on God and an involvement of others are both necessary components, no matter the context of ministry you find yourself. Remove the Lone Ranger title as soon as you can. Cast the net wide and involve others. The ministry will benefit, the leader will benefit, and those involved will as well. And to God be the glory.

Learning-to-action exercise

1) Provide details below to help shape the context of a sports ministry.

What is the size of the congregation? How many members?	
What facilities are available to the church for the use of recreation? Are they located on the church property? *(Note: the church does not have to own the facility for it to be available for use)*	
Programming – What programs/initiatives are currently a part of the sports and recreation ministry of the church?	
Community needs – What recreational needs can be identified within community?	

Performing a personal SWOT analysis

2) Perform a personal SWOT analysis. Remember, strengths and weaknesses embody the your internal and are likely to have direct control over, and opportunities and threats embody the external characteristics available that an individual may not have direct control over.

	STRENGTHS	**WEAKNESSES**
Internal		
	OPPORTUNITIES	**THREATS**
External		

CHAPTER SIX

LEADING COACHES

How to Approach Coach Recruiting, Training & Retention

Bob Schindler
Executive Director – Church Sports Outreach
Huntersville, NC
@SportsOutreach

Two of my favorite coaches are Coach Thompson, my community league football coach, and Coach Neely, my college golf coach. They were very different but I loved and respected them greatly.

Coach Thompson was a big and tough man (maybe all men seem big to a 10-year-old!). He had a shaved head long before it was cool. He inspired me and pulled out of me good things I did not even know existed. You might say I almost feared him (to this day I do not know what his first name is.), but his wife was my third grade teacher and his son played on the team so I knew he was human.

Coach Neely on the other hand was gentle and kind. He coached college football for 40 years at Southwestern, Clemson, and Rice Universities, winning 207 games and ranking 26th for career wins among major schools. He had long since retired from his football days when I encountered him as the Vanderbilt University AD Emeritus and Head Golf Coach. He never taught us much about golf but we learned about playing a game and about trust as he insisted upon driving us to all matches. I just loved being around him. He told the best stories and inspired me to be like him. I was blessed to have two great coaches and I smile thinking about them today. Both impacted me very positively.

What if every one of your coaches had such a positive influence on the players in your sports outreach initiatives? God would be glorified and He would use your ministry in marvelous ways. Sadly, the reality is such coaches are hard to find. In fact, one of the great challenges, if not the greatest challenge, sports ministers face is leading coaches—which includes: the recruiting, training, and retaining of coaches (or "Key Volunteers"). This is true for all coaches and much more for quality coaches like Coach Thompson or Neely.

The difficulty of recruiting, training & retaining coaches

There are several reasons why the leading of coaches is such a challenge. One of them is that ***recruiting*** volunteer coaches is never ending. Every new season typically brings with it the call for new coaches. To illustrate this struggle to other church staff, I ask those staff to imagine a conversation between the Pastor and the person leading the Children's Ministry. For example, it is the summer, when recruiting for teachers is at its pinnacle. The Pastor asks, "How is recruiting going?" The Leader responds, "Ok. It's just hard to get people to make a nine-month commitment these days. You know how busy everyone is." The Pastor responds, "I have a great idea. How about rather than a nine-month commitment, we reduce it to three months. However, that means every three months you have to re-recruit all your teachers. Oh, yeah, and also, every three months we would re-assign all classrooms and all students. What do you think?" The Leader promptly says, "I quit!!!!!" This untenable rhythm for any clear-thinking Children's Ministry leader is precisely what most Sports Ministers live with, making this recruiting and training not only a never ending process but daunting challenge.

Recruiting volunteer coaches should not be taken for granted. The recruitment process should begin 60-90 days prior to the start of the season.

In addition to the relentless pursuit of coaches, there is the sense that the supply seems so much smaller in the face of this demand. There are those who contend this is not just a perception. "Changes in society and cultural norms may hinder commitment and participation, creating pressures that make people less willing to volunteer" (Thumma & Bird, 2011). Even the competition for volunteers among ministries of the church can add to the problem.

In the face of such a formidable challenge, the question arises, "What can I do to recruit, train, and retain quality coaches?" You might be asking that question from a bit of a hopeless perspective that sees these challenges as almost unconquerable. Yet, you hope for something different or you would not be reading this chapter. You have in mind a ministry full of quality coaches. This vision is what draws you to this chapter, that along with the reality of challenges to living out this vision. In the light of that hope, you are genuinely asking this question with a desire for real insight into empowering coaches. My hope is that this chapter will leave you encouraged and equipped to more effectively handle your recruiting and ***training*** of coaches, which would then flow into your greater retention of them. My prayer is that God would work in and through your efforts in the years to come to rise up a team of such impactful coaches for your ministry.

Training of volunteers is often taken for granted, especially in coaching. Coaches need to know and understand the mission and vision of your faith community and the values you want to instill in your participant before all else. The technical side of coaching comes next.

Before looking more closely into these ideas, there are a couple of qualifications that are necessary. First of all, recruiting, training, and retaining coaches are not three independent ideas, but rather they need to work together to keep the coaches coming back year after year. Secondly, the recruiting, training, and developing of people is something I am passionate about. I have invested 30 years of my life focused on these concepts. In a short chapter like this, these ideas may come across simplistic or easy, but through my experience indicates they are neither. Giving yourself to others for their growth requires great sacrifice, has seasons of real disappointment, and will require the strength only God can supply. Yet, if the example of the One who gave Himself completely for our rescue and growth, our Great Leader Jesus, we find His joy to be our joy which empowers us to take on such challenges.

[6] A "Key Volunteer" is someone who shoulders the responsibility for implementing the vision of the Sports Ministry on the field, the court, or wherever the ministry takes place. He or she is the one who actually puts the vision into practice. In Youth Leagues, the Key Volunteers are referred to as Coaches. In Adult Leagues, they are often called Captains. Regardless of the title or Sports Ministry initiative, the principles in this chapter apply to these "Key Volunteers."

Recruiting

The Typical Way

I meet and talk with sports ministers on a regular basis…more than a handful every week. The subject of recruiting coaches comes up—a lot. When it does, I start to ask questions. The first one I usually ask is, "How do you recruit coaches?" The answers I most often hear begin with:

> ***"I go to previous coaches."***
> ***"I ask parents of players."***
> ***"I put announcements in the church bulletin/website."***

These answers deal primarily with the WHO the sports minister recruits.

"I want to know more about the HOW." I usually probe further, "Ok, but how do you recruit? What do you say when you are addressing those parents or those previous coaches or when you write those announcements?"

In these discussions, sports ministers say they typically recruit by the following:

> ***"Here is an opportunity for you to spend time with your kids."***
> ***"You love (a sport) and if you coach you have a chance to be around it."***
> ***"We have a waiting list of players. If you don't coach, those players won't get to play and won't be exposed to the spiritual content we offer."***

After listing these out, I usually point out that the way someone recruits flows out of what they believe about why people coach and what makes a ministry successful. To illustrate this connection, I then ask, "Why do you think adults agree to coach?" The answers that come up most frequently are:

"The want to spend time with my kids who are on the team."
"They love the sport."
"They want to have an impact."
"Because I was asked."

I point these reasons back to what they said about how they recruit to show the tie between how they recruit and why people coach.

The reason I do all this is to try to demonstrate the orientation or center of their recruiting. If a sports minister starts with an appeal to the needs of parents or the players, this recruiting approach can very easily become "Child" or "Parent" or "Coach" centered without the sports minister even realizing it.

To go a little deeper, I might ask, "What are the marks of a successful sports ministry and sports minister?" This is when things can get really interesting. Most of the time, the person I am interacting with is pretty foggy on their thinking here. (This is not just a problem just for sports ministers. I have found the same to be true for Pastors and Ministers in general and something I struggled with significantly during my years as a pastor.) Without realizing this, the fog can lead them to adopt something close to the world's ideas that says "bigger is better" or "success is never getting smaller."

From that underlying belief come such statements (spoken or unspoken) as:

> ***"If we don't have a certain number of teams (especially equal or more than a previous season), we are not a successful sports ministry."***
>
> ***"We can't be known as a ministry that turns people away."***
>
> ***"If I say no to those players and families because I don't have a coach for that team, I am a failure as a leader."***

If I see or sense this going on, we talk about the connection to the pressure they feel to recruit, the almost desperate attitude they have when approaching recruiting, and their beliefs about themselves and ministry success.

I try to point out for the same reason I do about the reasons people coach. If a sports minister starts with his or her needs or the needs of the ministry, what often happens is that, again probably without realizing it, the recruiting approach centers on himself or herself or the sports ministry.

In either case—this Child/Parent/Coach Centered or this Sports Minister/Ministry Centered (what we might combine and call Self-Centered)—the recruiting usually ends up pressure filled and manipulative in the recruiting attempts toward these self-centered ends.

A Better Way

To further this discussion, I ask sports ministers to consider the following question, "What would recruiting look like if it was Gospel centered instead?" (Carson & Keller, 2011). I love to have that conversation. Another way of asking the question is "If the Gospel is The Story of God's redemption of people and creation through Jesus Christ, what would recruiting look like if this Story of the Gospel was at the center?" It may sound like a simple shift but the results are profound. Beliefs about coaching would change to something like:

> ***"Coaching is an opportunity to be involved in God's plan of the redemption of people and sports."***

> ***"Coaching is a possibility for this person to fulfill the destiny God has in mind for that person."***

> ***"Coaching is not something people don't want to do. Having an impact through coaching is something they want to do, that God may have placed deep in their hearts."***

A transformation in the recruiting efforts would follow. Rather than being self-centered, these efforts will be God centered. *They will be:*

Inviting	**NOT**	**Begging**
Confident	**NOT**	**Desperate**
Assertive	**NOT**	**Apologetic**
Sensitive	**NOT**	**Pushy**
Grace-filled	**NOT**	**Guilt driven**
Full of prayer	**NOT**	**Full of worry**

Gospel centered recruiting invites people to play a part in God's Grand Gospel Story, rather than settle for the smaller stories of the sports minister or the coach. It highlights the impact of a coach's involvement in the sports ministry and the contribution they could make to The Story of the Gospel. It is sensitive to everyone involved and trusting God and not themselves or others for the desired impact.

When I look at Jesus and his recruiting, it seems that this is how he recruited. As he was forming his team of disciples (i.e., leaders), he said things like "Come, follow me and I will make you fishers of men" (Matthew 4:19). I see three components to his recruiting here. First, he gave an invitation, "Follow me." Second, he showed the impact of what they would become through accepting the invitation, "fishers of men." Third, he specified his role as the developer, "I will make." He did not invite them into a position. He invited them into a process, a process of development, which leads us to our next topic, training.

Conclusion

Before we talk about training, let me ask you a question. As you watch Jesus and his recruiting, does your heart long to be such a recruiter? Does your heart long to be someone with such grace and confidence? To be someone that understands the people he or she is recruiting will never regret accepting the invitations that God is in. Becoming this kind of recruiter begins with being passionate about what you do in addition to recognizing the orientation of our recruiting. It means turning from the typical self-centered approaches and moving toward a Gospel Centered approach to recruiting.

As we do so, rather than apologize for asking for these kinds of commitments, we need to boldly call people to them. Amidst the commitment-shy culture we live in, there is the need for such invitations. "Perhaps as never before, physical, tangible and meaningful commitments must be called for and nurtured—including at church" (Thumma & Bird, 2011).

Training

The Typical Way

I did not understand much about the broader sports ministry movement for the first 18 years of my sports ministry involvement. I started and led a sports ministry at the first church I served in as the Associate Pastor of Outreach. God guided me to work with my first church to then serve as the ***Church Planter*** and Pastor of a new church. In this second church, sports were our primary means of outreach—adults, kids, men, women, in mostly traditional sports—but I did not know many others or talked with anyone else about sports ministry during those years.

Church planter is an individual that works in a local community where their primary goal is to establish a new church.

Besides my questions about recruiting, I had another question in mind. I wanted to know what these sports ministers did to train their coaches. Because of my passion for developing people and even the limited perspective I had on sports ministry, I realized that a league-filled sports ministry would only advance on the shoulders of the coaches. In the light of that perspective, I asked sports ministers, "What do you do to train your coaches?" The answers I got were shocking. The best responses I heard were:

"We get coaches together for 2 hours on a Saturday once a season."

Remember, this answer was the best. Many said much less. I also asked them to show me what ***resources*** they gave to their coaches. Years behind the technology of the day, these materials reinforced the minimalist attitude toward the training and the importance of the coaches.

Resources in this context often refer to coaches' manuals, practice and game schedules, church policies and sports equipment. Really anything that would support a coach in what they do.

To understand further the status of training in this sports ministry movement, I also asked each one, including this best case, "What is the agenda of those Coach Meetings?" The typical answer came "We spend some time casually getting to know each other, go over rules and logistics, hand out uniforms." In the best case I heard, the last 15 minutes of the meeting would involve going over something about prayer or devotionals." Fifteen minutes on integrating sports and Christianity…once a season…that was the best.

Mission or mission statement will give clarity for any sports ministry program. The statement will reveal what the program provides participants and the fundamental reasons why your sports ministry exists.

The problems of such an approach was evident. Coaches either quit coming to these kinds of meetings or quit coaching all together, out of frustration for their lack of support or lack of growth.

A Better Way

I have been on a mission to change this culture, one that heralds a Gospel Centered approach to recruiting and development. It is an approach where the recruiting includes an invitation to enter into a process—a Development Process that acknowledges the significant competencies a coach must possess and enables them to grow in those competencies.

Vision or vision statement expresses what a sports ministry program would like to achieve within the next 3-5 years.

To illustrate the significance of these competencies, I ask sports ministers to list on a white board the characteristics of an *"Ideal Coach"*:

> ***What does the Ideal Coach need to know?***
> ***What does the Ideal Coach need to be able to do?***
> ***What does the Ideal Coach need to be?***

Consider these questions for a moment. An Ideal Coach would know about sports, not just the athletic aspects but how to be involved in redeeming those sports, know about your ministry—the ***mission*** and ***vision*** , know about first aid. An Ideal coach would be able to communicate with children, able to develop those children, know how to integrate Christianity into those sports during practice and games, how to run those practices and games. An Ideal Coach would be humble, loving, patient, and have a growing relationship with Christ, and be responsible. Just to get started. One

Vision statements can be as short as one sentence expressing the overarching goals of the program.

sports minister and his staff, after going through this exercise, realized none of them were qualified to coach if they had to measure up to these characteristics. This is where the process comes in. The list is not a list of characteristics a person must possess in order to coach but the characteristics you are helping them to become through the developmental process you have invited them into.

You may notice I did not call it a training process. I have a specific reason for that distinction. By definition, training is limited to the action of teaching a person a particular skill or type of behavior. Training to be complete usually involves a teaching and an observation component. A Gospel Centered process recognizes the various aspects of a person and involves the development of not just skill but knowledge and character as well. The diagram below describes developmental process I have developed over the years that is described as the Developmental Triangle. Developing coaches can be summarized in three areas, all-working together through a process.

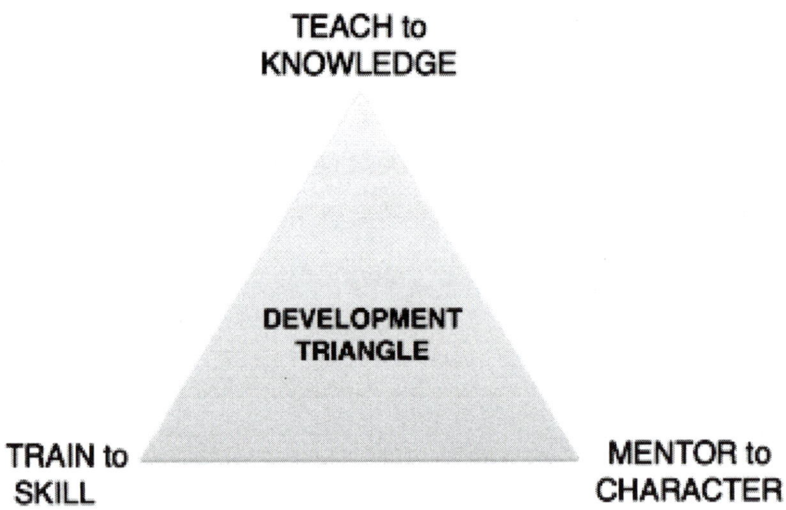

Teach to Knowledge: Teach what a Coach needs to know
Train to Skill: Train him or her in what they need to do
Mentor to Character: Mentor them to become Ideal Coaches

---

[7] For a list of these characteristics, contact CSO at info@csosports.org.
[8] For examples and additional resources regarding mission and vision statements, see appendix at end of this chapter.

Once a sports minister has these Ideal Coach characteristics in mind and recognizes the realities of the Development Triangle, he or she is ready to begin the process that bridges each of the points of the Triangle to work together. This is a learning opportunity, for the sports ministry and the coach.

Every learning environment has an atmosphere. Recognizing this as reality, calls us to try to put in place a Gospel Centered atmosphere for the Developmental Triangle. That atmosphere would accept the fact that no one ever arrives at the end. This is a continual process. Just as God continually sanctifies us into the image (the Knowledge, Skill and Character) of his Son, so we sports ministers co-labor with God to continually develop our coaches.

This ongoing Developmental Triangle process assumes the possibility of failure. Just as God promises us that "there is no condemnation for those in Christ Jesus" (Romans 8:1) in our failures in the process of us becoming more like Jesus. So, sports ministers need to create an atmosphere that accepts and does not reject coaches as they fail to be these kind of people.

Accepting failure does not mean it is not addressed. Grace is the key deliverable in handling failure. This is where the Ideal Coach characteristics are so helpful. These characteristics are the agreed-upon standard to which coaches are called. In a grace-filled atmosphere, failure can be discussed and seen as justification for further development. Coaches are embraced in their acknowledged failure as the sports minister demonstrates his or her desire to help the coach become someone better.

Progress is celebrated.

The Psalmist says,

Great is the Lord and worthy of praise, his greatness no one can fathom. One generation will commend you works to another; they will tell of his mighty acts…they will celebrate his abundant goodness and joyfully sing of his righteousness. (Psalm 145:3-7).

Jesus said, *"I will make you fishers of men."* He is the one authoring all transformation. He uses all kinds of vehicles including the Developmental Process a sports minister has in place. His work is the focus of such recognition in the life of a coach.

Community is key to this recognition. Everybody wants to grow, but we do not often recognize the progress God is bringing about in us until someone who knows us points it out, so with coaches. They need others to show their progress. They need you the sports minister and they need other coaches as well to do this. Facilitating the growth of such a community of coaches, where they become a real "team" helping each other make progress toward the "Ideal Coach," needs to be considered when looking at the structure for the Developmental Process.

Conclusion

My least favorite coach was my High School football coach, Coach Smith (a pseudonym). The summer of my sophomore year, my family went on a summer vacation. We were scheduled to come back 3 days after summer football practices began. I asked a good friend to tell the coach I would miss those practices. My athletic career trajectory was significantly altered when I showed up for practice. My friend forgot to tell the coach why I was late. He thought I was acting like a "prima donna" and wanted to make an example of me. His tirade lasted all through the two-a-day practices and had such an impact that I never played another down of my favorite sport, having played for eight years previously. Coaches impact their players. God promises through the Developmental Triangle to turn your Coaches, who may be like Coach Smith, into ones that are beloved by their players like Coach Thompson and Coach Neely. While there are great challenges to putting in place such a Developmental Process, the question for you is will you trust him, accept the challenge, and begin to implement such a Developmental Triangle, one that sees more and more Coach Neely's rather than Coach Smith coach in your ministry?

Retention

To this point, I have covered recruiting and training and shown how they integrate through the Developmental Triangle. As we turn to the topic of ***retention***, we see a similar integration. Gospel centered recruiting and training impacts retention. If you have recruited coaches to this vision of Kingdom impact; if you have helped coaches through your developmental process; if you have lead your coaches in understanding the impact coaches have on participants; then it would follow that these coaches would want to stay with the ministry. Retention is addressed by the implementation of these ideas on recruiting and training. By working with your Coaches, they will see that you care about what they do for you and for the participants.

Retention is the act of keeping a coach within your sports ministry program throughout the season. Retaining a coach shows the willingness for a coach to come back next year.

There are several points that need to be emphasized to strengthen that retention. First of all, coaches need to see progress. Researchers tell us that 66% of Christians in the US think they are plateaued or declining in their spiritual growth (Pew Research Center, 2015). All Christians want to grow but only a third think they are. The same is true for coaches. As the sports minister, you need to provide them means to grow and then show them the growth to tap into this desire to grow and alleviate this frustration. I often hear from sports ministers that coaches do not have the time for this kind of training. In over 30 years of working with people, many of whom are coaches, I have found that people will make time for growth. If a proven process for growth is put before them, engagement in that process takes place, and progress is recognizing, people will make time for this engagement, even if that time requirement increases. Most often, what a coach is telling you when they say they do not have time is either:

> He or she does not agree with the person you want them to become. They have a different vision for a Coach. They think they can be much less and still coach. They are fine and do not need the Developmental Triangle.

[9] Many churches actual use the Ideal Coach characteristics, even in the form of a Job Description, when it recruits Coaches. They are placed before a potential coach and the coach is asked, "Where do you see yourself as competent in these characteristics and where do you see yourself lacking?" This leads to a discussion about the Developmental Process, including the specifics of that process that further ties recruiting and training together.

They do not believe the process of the Development Triangle will bring growth.

They do not see any personal progress through that process.

If the vision is agreed upon and the process brings recognized growth, people will hang around. This is not to say everyone who is ever recruited and developed will be a life-long coach. If people walked away from the greatest inviter and developer the world has ever seen, they will certainly walk away from the lesser likes of us. The second intensifier of Gospel centered retention is this development community emphasized in the previous section. We all struggle. We all should share the struggle together. Struggling with others is certainly better than struggling alone. We have a built in support group of sport ministry coaches, we are in together to support each other that may struggle. This support turns the struggle in to growth as a sport ministry coach and leader.

Conclusion

Leading Coaches, may be, one of the greatest challenge as a sports minister. Hopefully, through this chapter you have gained encouragement and direction to further tackle those challenges that surround recruiting, training, and retaining Coaches. My prayer is that God would inspire, lead, and use you in new ways to become "fishers of men" in the realm of sports ministry and experience the joys, amidst the challenges, of such a ministry among great coaches.

Learning-to-action exercise

Recruiting

1. Based on this chapter, what are three talking points that you would focus on when you recruit a coach to be a part of your sports ministry?

b)____

c)____

d)____

Training

2. Based on this chapter, what are three training aspects that you would focus on when training your coaches to be a part of your sports ministry? Why?

a. ____

Why? ______________________________________

____

b.____

Why?______________________________________

____

c.____

Why?______________________________________

Retention

3. Based on this chapter, what are three talking points that you would focus on when you are discussing with your coach about staying with the sports ministry program?

a)____

b)____

c)____

Appendix A

Mission = Destination or where you are going.

Mission statement examples

To combine the gift of leisure with the companionship of Christ
Cool Spring Recreation Ministry – Mechanicsville, VA
Use sport and recreation to love God, love people, share Jesus, and make disciples.

Bellevue Baptist Church Youth Sports Program – Memphis, TN
Loving and leading people to Jesus through sports and recreation

Crestwood Church Recreation Ministries – Richmond, VA
OARS (Outer Annapolis Recreation & Sports) is a new ministry of Riva Trace Baptist Church looking to connect people of all ages in the Annapolis area with God and one another through a wide variety of traditional and nontraditional sports and recreation.

Riva Trace Baptist Church Outer Annapolis Recreation & Sports Ministry – Davidsonville, MD

Vision = Path or how you will get there.

Vision statement examples

We are an outreach-focused ministry seeking to connect people of all ages in the Annapolis area with God and one another through a wide variety of traditional and non-traditional sports and recreation.

-quality programs and coaching
-safe and fun activities
-emphasis on teamwork, character and sportsmanship

Riva Trace Baptist Church Outer Annapolis Recreation & Sports Ministry – Davidsonville, MD

Engage Christ Covenant membership to participate in our outreach ministry by promoting and building redemptive relationships with SOAR families in our local community thru sports leagues, camps, clinics, and recreational activities.

Provide youth, adults and families of all abilities an atmosphere of Christ-centered competition, which teaches about sports, life, and the Gospel.

Encourage non-churched participants to move from the field into our church community.

-Use both Christ Covenant facilities and off campus sites to host events year round.

- Christ Covenant Church – SOAR Sports – Matthews, NC

CHAPTER SEVEN

MARKETING
within the Local Church Sports Ministry

Greg English
Recreation Minister
Compass Sports
Cool Spring Baptist Church
Mechanicsville, VA
CSRM Board of Trustee Chair
@recreatn

Jimmy Smith, Ph.D.
Assistant Professor
Sport Management
School of Education
Gonzaga University
Spokane, WA
@JimmySmithPhD
@SportsMinWins

Once you open your mouth to talk to someone about your sports ministry program you are marketing. Once you send that email, once you make that phone call, once you make a flyer, once you make an announcement in your church about the happenings of your sports ministry, you are marketing.

We would argue that every chapter that you read in this handbook has some component of marketing too it…recruiting coaches, managing conflict, training your staff…people are watching, people are perceiving, and people are making decisions (positively and negatively) about your sports ministry…and then…people talk to their friends and they talk about your sports ministry program. Well… marketing your program may not be as easy as the above mentions, but hopefully you can see that marketing is necessary for growth and sustainability for your sports ministry program. Having a plan to get the word out about your program is critical for continued growth of participation and revenues throughout the years your program exists.

Marketing encompasses all that we see on a daily basis. Advertising, promotions, TV commercials, sponsorship, public relations, and especially branding are all forms of marketing. Communicating your messages in the form of marketing techniques is a difficult task. Any time there is a message that is to be delivered between the Sender (the sport minister) and the Receiver (i.e., current and future participants and other stakeholders of the ministry such as community members) you are marketing. The success of your sports ministry lies with the how you deliver the message…the story…about your program. Sport ministers must be aware that a disruption of the messages can often occur. This is why having a plan for your sports ministry programs marketing efforts is essential…and it begins with your story. Brand marketing expert, Jeremy Darlow, who is a marketing executive for adidas, has worked with some of the most recognizable intercollegiate athletic departments in the United States like Notre Dame, University of Michigan, and UCLA. Jeremy highlighted in his book *Brands Win Championships* that writing your story and telling your story is the key for just about any sport organization to build a successful brand. To understand branding from a broad sport organization perspective, we encourage you to pick up Mr. Darlow's book, it is a great read and extremely informative. We both use this book in the courses we teach. In the meantime, we have provided you with some practical experience as Greg has recently gone through a branding change with his sports ministry and these experiences will aid in the building of your brand.

Branding

A **brand** includes but is not limited to a name, logo, or symbol associated with a sport organization (Pitts & Stotlar, 2013).

Often times the marketing and the ***branding*** aspects of building a sports ministry "take a back seat" because many sport ministers either do not have much experience with marketing, or simply do not have time. The result of a lack of marketing results in sports ministers or volunteers left wondering why no one knows about the opportunities or the vision of integrating sports and faith of your sports ministry program throughout the community. The consequence then becomes an inconsistent and often skewed perception of the programs you offer as well as the what your sport ministry program is trying to accomplish. Marketing your sports ministry may be one of the most important aspects to building your program inside and outside your community. When you properly market your ministry, you are building a positive perception and culture; and you are building a brand. Write your story and tell your sports ministry program's story…share your short term and long-term vision of your ministry with all who will listen.

Cool Spring Recreation branding case study

I (Greg) have been a part of two branding and marketing campaigns with Cool Spring Recreation. Not long after my arrival to Cool Spring, I began to see and hear the impact that the Recreation Center and its sports ministry was having on the community. While it had a name, "The Rec Center," it was evident that a "brand" was necessary for further development and expansion. The projects included the branding of the recreation facility and overall ministry and the re-branding of a youth sports program. Each project had its own uniqueness and occurs at different times, but both had numerous questions that needed to be answered and extensive ***market research*** was necessary to take on a branding effort such as this.

The essence of **market research** is to collect information about your consumer's needs and preferences. Primary research finds you conducting surveys, speaking with focus groups, or conducting one on one interviews. Secondary research is utilizing databases to find more information about your participants such as spending patterns or extracurricular activities they may take part in.

After being open to the public for twelve years and continually hearing people say "I am going to the Rec Center," our staff and team decided we wanted to accompany the "Rec Center" slogan with an image that would represent our brand visually as well as verbally. This would be similar to how Nike utilizes the slogan "Just Do It" with its Swoosh logo. In order to accomplish this, market research was necessary to further understand how we as well as the community perceived our brand identity. After several months, the primary theme from the research was eye opening. The community identified the "Rec Center" as a place people could move their bodies with their own individual goals in addition to the opportunity

Your **brand identity** may be strong or weak based on the ability of your consumer to recognize your name, logo or symbol used in your marketing campaign.

to participate in team goals. This was not far from what our staff viewed as well. So, we began to look at the development of a ***brand identity*** with these two ideas:

(1) movement or motion and

(2) continued pursuit of personal and/or team goals

Along with these two ideas, the team at Cool Spring Recreation also felt it was important to incorporate the overall mission of the church and recreation ministry.

The staff and team felt the above logo reflected the views of those participating and shared the biblical mission for discipling people in the areas of finishing well and striving towards the eternal.

Re-branding

After several years of success with the new brand identity, Cool Spring began to embark into uncharted territory. A partnership blossomed with an outside church sports ministry to provide programming that Cool Spring would see growth in its youth league participation and its volunteers. After several years, and the observing of the ever-changing local culture of youth sports, the Cool Spring team continued to expand through the development of its own materials for coach development and league play. Things were changing, in a blessed and positive direction. This natural progression, did however, show the need for a re-evaluation of the current Cool Spring brand. The challenge ahead was not only to celebrate the past, but also to introduce our change in responsibility and direction to our community. Our team felt that identity was evolving enough that a name and brand change was necessary to show a reflection of these changes already taking place. We went through a similar process when establishing Cool Spring. We continued to research our own identity perception with our members and community all while continuing to tell our story and vision both verbally and visually through our logo. The result would be the creation of Compass Sports. The Compass communicates both verbally and artistically a gospel-focused sports ministry. As we began to introduce the new brand, we did so with a gospel-centered sports design. At the core of the recreation ministry we desired to see all participants growing in their relationship to Christ and their skill and abilities in sports. Cool Spring Recreation uses a sports ministry map grid that provides accountability of the spiritual and athletic direction of persons involved within the programming. It works as a compass for providing direction to Christ and the local church. The arrow within the compass strives to point northward, knowing that we all fall short of God's glory and cannot achieve that without salvation and sanctification. It was important for us as a staff and team to be able to represent a brand and logo that both the mission and vision of integration of faith and sports could be explained.

COMPASS SPORTS

How did Cool Spring/Compass Sports do it?

Initial questions should be asked when considering branding or re-branding efforts for your sports ministry program. The sports minister and team need to see the need and purpose toward these efforts. Branding is more than artwork and design, it is seeing the bigger picture and how or why the creation or change in brand or name can better represent the ministry to all, internal of the ministry and externally. Spending time with ministry leaders, volunteers,

[10] The gird has a horizontal line which processes the development of the athlete or fan / spectator and vertical line that processes the discipleship and relationship with Christ throughout the athletes or fans involvement in sport. To learn more about this grid, see McCown and Gin (2003) publication.

and participants can help you understand your current position and comprehension of whether a creation of or change is needed. Asking these individuals their perception of the ministry, how would they describe the ministry, what words best describe the ministry, can refine your branding efforts. Defining a brand by developing an image that represents your sports ministry can provide purpose for those that work in the ministry and enhance recognition by those wanting to find a ministry that suits their faith needs.

Asking the right questions

Any research will welcome and seek out the difficult questions. Rather than asking questions that appeal to your desires, ask the questions that discover your past and can point toward the future.

Here are several questions for the sports minister and sports ministry team to work through:

Describe your sports ministries brand?
How would others describe your brand?
If you have an existing brand image, is it outdated or misleading? (Ask others)
Does your brand represent the mission and vision of your church and sports ministry?
Who needs to be involved in your branding or rebranding?
What is the timeframe?

Working with the Cool Spring Recreation staff and team through these questions took serious reflection and time. When presenting these discussions, your sports minister and team will need to script out the answers. In doing so, the ministry can discover its past, strengths, weaknesses, opportunities, and threats (Refer to Chapter 5 for a detailed discussion of SWOT analysis...remember a SWOT analysis can be utilized for individuals as well as sport organizations). Throughout the process, use the creation of or change in brand as a time of celebration to create momentum toward the future of a new brand.

Establish a timeline

Timing is critical, a marketing or brand introduction that happens too fast can leave your audience behind and confused, and a marketing or brand introduction that takes too long can create uncertainty. As Cool Spring worked through its timeline, the team set specific dates during the weeks that involved specific tasks each day and checkpoints during the weeks and upcoming months to be completed to build up to the marketing strategy and branding reveal.

When creating a timeline, start with the end in mind. Knowing your desired reveal date and marketing efforts after this date will permit you to work backwards towards an effective start date. As Cool Spring began its process, the staff and team knew they wanted to launch the brand of youth leagues by the registration date of the basketball season. With a date being set for September, the timeline was set back six months to February, more time probably would have helped, but less time would have certainly been a rush.

Each sports ministry will need to determine their level of aggressiveness in relation to their target audiences and how to best develop their timeline. These timelines can be weaved in to the marketing plan steps below. Even before beginning the development of a marketing plan, consider the following to ease the challenge of developing and implementing a marketing strategy to the public.

Invite a task force of staff and volunteers (3-5 people) within the sports ministry to discuss, write out, and define answers to key questions noted above.

Contact, invite and possibly hire a marketing specialist or someone within the field of marketing to serve within the task force. This person will provide feedback and suggestions as the team moves through the process. In an effort to stay at a professional level on a non-professional marketing budget, Cool Spring invited two marketing professionals to serve and join the team to create a brand that would impact families and individuals of the community. We invited them into something bigger than just a job; we invited them into an opportunity of influence and service. Their role was to provide copy review of materials and education on the "how" to get the word out in various formats. It was a role that they felt invested in, but not overwhelmed by, and Cool Spring benefitted with a professional outcome and product. I also would recommend my co-author (Dr. Jimmy Smith) to provide such a service as he has had experience in the branding and re-branding efforts of several sport organizations. Additional support available from the Association of Church Sports and Recreation Ministries (csrm.org).

Assign specific tasks to specific people. On the team, there will be people with key skills. Understanding what skills each member has can be a huge asset and potentially expedite this process and will make your program much more efficient and effective. As you will see below in the steps in building a marketing plan, you can easily assign one step to one person on the task force. This specializes that person on the task and refines their focus in the overall efforts of the marketing plan.

Meet with and hire a graphic designer. Share the answers of the key questions with the graphic designer and allow creative time for them to develop an artistic concept that portrays the verbal message. Give them as much information about the sports ministry, the church, its people and your community.

The timeline that was established by Cool Spring Recreation included specific dates and times that were set for each one of the communication vehicles (i.e., verbal, print, social media) to be used as well as what would be communicated through them. Communication processes need to be strategic and have purpose. You want people to see, hear, and experience the purpose and vision of your brand. Utilizing the below marketing plan template can guide you down this path.

---

[11] Visit the Association of Church Sports and Recreation Ministries (CSRM) at http://www.csrm.org/

Start your sports ministry marketing strategy here

Developing a marketing plan will be the blueprint that outlines your sports ministry programs marketing efforts over the course of a season or year. This may include marketing new branding efforts as noted above, or simply marketing the start of a new youth basketball league. The plan should describe the activities involved in accomplishing specific marketing tasks within a set time frame. Remember, conducting as much research to prepare these below tasks is critical.

Task #1 - *Creating a value for your sports ministry program*

You have a story, you have a brand, you have a timeline, but what you may not have is value. What value do you bring to the potential participants? ***Creating value*** for what your sport ministry have to offer is necessary. Whether you like this terminology or not, your participants are consumers and being able to identify your consumer's needs will bring them in the door to your ministry. Creating value suggests that you understand the marketing concepts of the "4-Ps."

Creating value are the benefits to satisfy the consumer's needs. Once you state the benefits you accept the responsibility to deliver this promise.

PRODUCT

What is the nature of what you are offering to the participant/consumer? Is it simply a place to play a sport...or is it more than this? The participant/consumer needs to know what you have to offer... specifically.

PRICE

A fair price that also reflects the image you want to portray about what you have to offer. Considerations include competitor's price.

PLACE

How do you intend to deliver what you have to offer? Is it at one site, or multiple sites? What are the transportation consequences for your staff and the consumer? How will the participant/consumer register? Make it as easy as possible.

PROMOTION

Getting your message out about what you have to offer to potential consumers. This can be attained through publicity, advertising, or other means of communication (see marketing strategy section below). Be creative!

Task #2 – ***Understanding the marketing environment***

You may be the only sports ministry program in the area, but you are certainly not the only sports program in the area with the YMCA, your cities recreation department and other little league offerings. Understanding your environment and how it affects your marketing plan could be considered the most important task to complete. As you can see in the figure below, a sports ministry program has direct environmental factors to consider and indirect environmental factors to consider. Those touching the sports ministry program box are direct environmental factors that you will manage on a regular, even daily, basis such as working with the senior pastor to inform them of the success and impact of your ministry (see Chapter 10 for assistance with this). Those not touching the sports ministry program box are occasional issues that should be addressed from time to time. Technology changes so often, the next social media craze I am sure is around the corner. An economic downturn can effect whether or not parents can pay for their kids to participate in your program. Understanding the demographic and cultural concerns in your area (i.e., age, gender, race) can affect participation rates. Legal issues can arise if you decide to take your ministry mobile .

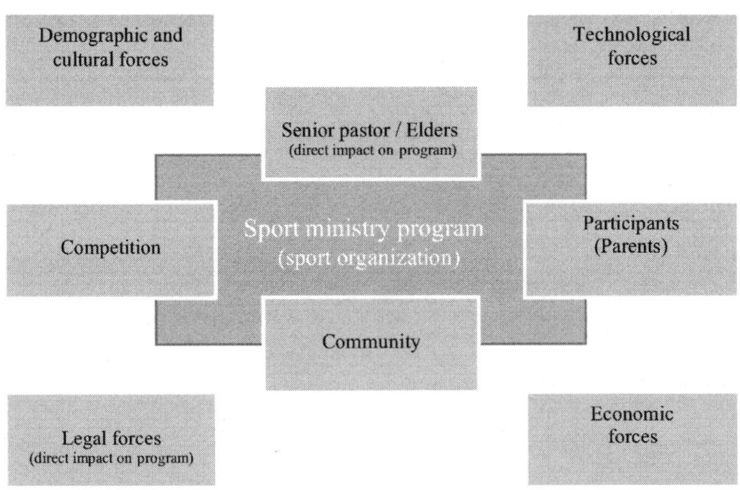

(The above diagram is derived from Pedersen, P & Thibault, L. (2007). *Contemporary Sport Management* (5th ed.). Human Kinetics Publishers).

Task #3 – *Target markets*

We have alluded to ***target markets*** throughout this chapter. Identifying your target market may be as simple as the sports, and level of sports you offer in your ministry. Targeting these levels may be all, some or one, but it is the levels that may need to be decided. Canadian Sport for Life, a government agency, promote Long-term Athletic Development (LTAD), a model developed seven stages for physical activity from birth the much later stages in life.

Target markets are the selection of consumer segments for which marketing strategies are developed. Popular segments are demographics (age, race, gender) or geographic and how far participants are willing to travel to your sport facility.

Stage 1: Active Start (0-6 years)
Stage 2: FUNdamentals (girls 6-8, boys 6-9)
Stage 3: Learn to Train (girls 8-11, boys 9-12)
Stage 4: Train to Train (girls 11-15, boys 12-16)
Stage 5: Train to Compete (girls 15-21, boys 16-23)
Stage 6: Train to Win (girls 18+, boys 19+)
Stage 7: Active for Life (any age participant)

The great perspective of the above stages is two-fold, first, each stage has an age range to target. Second, each stage has a value proposition such as FUNdamentals or Learn to Train. We encourage you to visit canadiansportforlife.ca and search LTAD to learn more about these stages, these stages may provide you with ideas as to what target market should be selected or even what you might specialize in at your sports ministry program. But remember, if you consider targeting children 12 years of age and under, you may not actually be marketing to these children, but their parents. They are the ones that have the means to sign their children up for sports and drive them to and from their practices and games. Selecting a younger age group is great, but show the value to the parents as well.

Task #4 – *Marketing objectives*

The idea of objectives is often used interchangeably with ***goals***, but in fact they are quite different. To be successful at achieving goals and objectives they need to be separated, where objectives are used

To expand on **goals** and objectives earlier in this handbook...Goals are a broad key outcome(s) for your sports ministry program. An objective is a measurable stepping stone you take to achieve stated goal(s).

[12] A sports ministry colleague has a mobile skateboard ministry that he takes from town to town in San Antonio, Texas. This is a wonderful and unique ministry and the value this ministry creates is second-to-none. However, the legal implications for something like this needs to be addressed. Injuries and damage to surrounding property are among a few concerns that need to be addressed.

to achieve goals. Objectives should be used as a stepping-stone to achieve another objective that will eventually result in reaching your goal. Clearly identifying these in your marketing plan will help guide the process and keep you on your timeline.

A common way to write out proper objective is to use the **SMART objective** approach.

SPECIFIC	*Be as exact as possible with your objective.*
MEASURABLE	*How do we measure the objective? If you are unable to measure it, then it may be a goal rather than an objective.*
ATTAINABLE/ ACHIEVABLE	*Can the objective be completed in a reasonable amount of time with the resources that currently exist within your sports ministry?*
RELEVANT/ REALISTIC	*Will this objective have a direct effect on the goal at hand?*
TIME BOUND	*When will this objective be accomplished. Be specific here. Exact dates (even times) are best.*

SMART objective examples:
Goal – ***To fill 20 youth basketball teams (age 11-16) for the winter season.***

Objectives #1:
To generate social media messages (both Facebook and Twitter) about the league once every other day alternating times (morning/evening), beginning 5 weeks before the season on January 15th.

Doran, G. T. (1981). "There's a S.M.A.R.T. Way to Write Management's Goals and Objectives," Management Review, Vol. 70, Issue 11, pp. 35-36.

Objective #2:

To activate past league and team participants via email to visit website to register by December 15th and receive a discount on team fees. (Emails will be sent on Black Friday, and then once a week until deadline.)

Task #5 – *Marketing strategies*

Communication comes in various formats when developing a strategy to get the word out about your sports ministry program and brand. Determine what ***marketing strategy*** and forms of communication will be most effective. Forms of communication to consider are:

Marketing strategies defines the exact procedures that a marketing plan will take to communicate to the consumer.

Verbal communication—people impacting people—word of mouth. One of the best ways for people to hear about the brand is through current participants. Whether they are involved in youth leagues, adult leagues, or fitness classes, it is important to recruit key families, coaches, and participants to tell others why they are excited about the ministry.

Social Media—Email, Constant Contact, Facebook, Twitter, Instagram. Determine what you currently use that is effective and what is one you could add that is missing as a way to communicate. Whatever you decide to use…be consistent…as this is the way that people with be informed by your ministry program. Frequency of your social media is also important, but be careful, being too frequent can often bother and event annoy your participants.

Promotional Items—determine if promotional give-a-ways will increase awareness. Anything from shirts, hats, to pens, and stickers can be used. When making this decision, ask around as to what promotional items will give you the best exposure. These do have a cost, so be cautious not to have promotional items just to have them.

Print—While it is not recommended as a primary form of communication, it may be useful to some populations. Please consider your sports ministry setting before utilizing print as a form of communication as the above options are so widely used, print may not be necessary. However, if print is a viable option these forms of print communication could be used: Fliers, posters, newspaper, magazine, signage, or community publications. When in doubt when dealing with marketing strategies...*be creative with your communication.*

Task #6 – *Evaluation*

The process of evaluation can be simple for some and challenging for others. The challenge lies with finding the time to evaluate your marketing plan. Often times if an evaluation occurs, many wait until the end of the marketing plan to evaluate the plan, which is fine, but sport ministry managers should consider the practice of evaluating along the way. What is successful and what is going to be something to improve upon the next time. Utilizing the timelines, you set as well as reaching your SMART objectives will prove to be good evaluation practices. Additional concepts of evaluation can be found in Chapter 4 of this handbook.

Start writing and sharing your story

The process of creating a brand or marketing strategy can be exciting. However, it does not happen without a plan, asking questions, doing research, and setting timelines. Even though Cool Spring stuck with its timeline for marketing and brand changes, it was certainly not complete, marketing and branding changes may never be 100% complete. The story of your ministry, the experiences of people involved, and the icon or logo must continue to be presented and communicated. This may be one area that affects the success of a sports ministry. Sports ministers need to think long term and recognize that in order to stay in front of potential audiences, a healthy competitive strategy will need to continue. While remaining true to the core of the mission and vision, the efforts of creativity will continue to adjust to the ever changing sports culture and its participants who typically look for the next event or program. Following the marketing plan tasks we have provided for you above will prove to be a good template for those looking to establish a marketing plan to promote their sports ministry brand. Please know, however, the tasks above are a good start, evolving your marketing strategy, plan and timeline are areas that can be adjusted to any given sport ministry program situation.

Marketing and branding begins with how you write your story and how you share that story. It is such a powerful way to communicate. Throughout scripture, from Genesis to Revelation, we find ourselves immersed in the details of God's story. In fact, it is through these stories that we understand the Why of God's purpose as well as the sense of feeling (meaning our senses are opened so that we can experience what is being said) through the specific details of stories that draws us into a deeper understanding, Jesus himself found it important to speak through stories or parables. If you study the process of Jesus from a marketing lens, you will find three areas of an impactful message. First, through these stories, the message or why was taught and demonstrated. Second, through these stories people were invited to participate. Third, through these stories lives were impacted and change occurred both spiritually and physically. Jesus himself understood the why and the importance of sharing it with others, he always included an invitation to be part of something greater, and offered the benefits of his invitation.

As you think about developing your story, think in terms of those participating. The greatest tool in marketing is word of mouth. While the use of social media and other formats is vital, typically when asked, "how did you hear about our programs or ministry" most answer with, "I was told by..." Your ideal marketing scenario is people participating within your ministry and talking about your ministry and program…they need to be a part of your primary marketing plan. Capture their stories. Their stories of why they participate, how it has changed them, why it is valuable to them (remember creating value is one of the tasks above), and what their participation in the ministry will do for others. What you are creating is really a re-branding approach of how God's story has been shared for over two thousand years.

We all have a story and we all have brand. It is the sports minister and recreation staff or team's responsibility to frame that story and communicate it to the outside. When you begin to understand your why or purpose and apply it to the specific impacts (recreation, fitness, or sports life changes) through a marketing strategy, you then have an impactful brand.

Learning to action activity

Branding

1. Write out your history or story of your recreation ministry. If you are a new sport minister, using key words or themes, what would your ideal story be for your new sports ministry program?

2. As you see key words of phrases arising from your story, what word, picture, or symbol represents these?

3. How do others describe their experience with your ministry? If new, talk to someone at a church and how they would perceive a sports ministry at their church.

SMART Goals and objectives

In the strategic planning process, goals and objectives should be established. It is often recommended that these satisfy the criteria known as SMART objective. (specific, measurable, achievable, realistic and time-bound).

Write one (1) goal here and two (2) or more SMART objectives to reach that goal.

SMART Goal / Objective #1

____

____

SMART Goal / Objective #2

____

____

Begin taking notes below on the tasks to start and build a sport ministry program marketing plan.

Marketing plan

1. Utilize the task headings below, take a few notes for each to get you started thinking about a marketing plan for your sports ministry based on this chapter readings.

Tasks	Notes
Creating a value proposition	
Understanding the marketing environment	
Target market	
Marketing objectives	
Marketing Strategies	
Evaluation	

CHAPTER EIGHT

SPORTS MINISTRY
Management with Limited Space

David Waddell
Lecturer – Parks and Recreation Management
University of Mississippi
CSRM Board of Trustee Member

The yard, despite my father's care, had four worn out places in a diamond shape. The spots represented first base, second base, third base, and home plate for the neighborhood wiffle ball games.

We lived in a neighborhood that had no access to a field or vacant lot, so our front yard became the place to play. Numerous times in my upbringing I had no basketball goal, baseball backstop, soccer net, or goal posts to aid me in my play. For basketball, a section of the roof that hung over the garage was designated as the basket. If a shot hit the small square of a shingle it counted as a goal. For goal posts a branch of a tree was utilized. The soccer net became the middle portion of the garage door just beneath the windows. My younger brother and I even designed portions of the game that could be played in our shared bedroom, one of which was what we called "First and Goal." One of us sat on the edge of our bed while the other had the football and had to cross the plane of the goal that was the wall on the other side of the bed. Dad never could figure out why the legs of our bed kept breaking so easily.

Basketball games have been played on driveways and playgrounds during the day and at night using car headlights to light up the court. People want to play; the lack of a specific facility does not mean the sport does not occur.

Basketball games have been played on driveways and playgrounds during the day and at night using car headlights to light up the court. People want to play; the lack of a specific facility does not mean the sport does not occur.

Precedent set

During my years in high school and college I was fortunate to attend a church that had a minister responsible for sports and recreation. This leader informed the church to hold off on building a facility until a program could be established. For five years I observed this church conducting numerous programs without having a facility to host one of them.

> An **internship** is an opportunity for individuals to gain hand-on experience in the sport industry. If you are looking for help with your sports ministry, there may be a sport management program near you to contact and offer an internship to an eager sport management student. There are more than 400 sport management programs around the North America. Visit North American Society for Sport management website for contact information. www.nassm.com

My course of study in college was in recreation administration that required me to do an eight-week ***internship*** whereby I worked full-time with an existing recreation program. I chose to work in a church without an established facility in order to continue my learning of programming without a building. My tenure in sports ministry included a variety of field and facility resources. During seminary I served in a church that had a gym, racquetball court, game room, and locker facilities. It also served as the auditorium for Sunday morning services. The first church I served following seminary had only a gymnasium to offer. The second church had a gym, game room, shower, and two softball fields. The third had a craft room, bowling lanes, gym, racquetball court, exercise room, locker room, and shower facilities. Finally, the fourth church I worked for had two gyms, an aerobics exercise room, fitness machines, cardio machines, two racquetball courts, locker rooms with Jacuzzis, craft room, snack area, game room, and a large lobby. There was also a four-field complex used for baseball, softball, and soccer. The complex had a playground and concession stand in the middle of the four fields. I felt like I was the apostle Paul in a sense when he said, Not that I am speaking of being in need, for I have learned in whatever situation I am to be content. I know how to be brought low, and I know how to abound. In any and every circumstance, I have learned the secret of facing plenty and hunger, abundance and need. (Philippians 4:11-12)

I have served churches without formal facilities and I have served churches with "Taj Mahal" facilities. Space is always of a concern for many sport programs and those who manage them. The search for facilities and a place to play has been a concern for sports ministry leaders since the program ministry was founded. The need is prevalent to secular organizations as well. One study, taken in urban areas, discovered informal sports were engaged in a variety of sports in empty lots or building spaces used primarily for different activities (Bach, 1993).

Foundations and formations

The creation of certain sports had nothing to do with the available facilities. James Naismith invented basketball so athletes could have something to do indoors. A peach basket was hung off a wall and required a ladder to get the ball after a successful shot (Laughead, 2014). Baseball was simply played in any available open space. What does a church or parachurch ministry do to evangelize or disciple people when there are no facility or limited facilities? This chapter will look at the sophistication of sports facilities. We will relate the sports ministry into a mission mindset and how facilities can often be more of a burden than a blessing for sports ministries. Finally, we will look at possible resources to host sports ministries outside of the traditional venues.

Sophistication of sports ministry facilities

In the early days of sports and recreation ministries to simply have a gymnasium meant you were at the top of the heap. When interviewing for a new position a candidate would ask, "Do you have a gym?" If the answer were positive the candidate would be im-

Effectiveness is the extent to which goals can be attained. (Steers & Black, 1994)

Efficiency is the cost and/or benefit ratio incurred in the pursuit of goals. (Steers & Black, 1994)

pressed. Sports ministry has now grown into such a viable ministry that we now ask how many fields, pools, and gymnasiums a church might own. A judgment is made on the ***effectiveness and efficiency*** of a program based on the size of a field space or facility. We no longer have boys and girls playing basketball in rag-tag T-shirts. Now they are all decked out in matching uniforms. The playing areas contain more than just a chain link backstop. They now resemble miniature stadiums. Score clocks and scoreboards must have all the newest "bells and whistles" or be considered second class.

The desire to become top-shelf or get to where we are putting on the Ritz has limited a number of churches and parachurch ministries into attempting to offer leagues and tournaments. I think churches and ministries should offer the best they can in facilities and fields, but it should not be the focal point of the ministry. There is no need to apologize if a facility is not the "Taj Mahal" of sports facilities. In the Gospel of Matthew, Jesus says, "Foxes have holes, and birds of the air have nests, but the Son of Man has nowhere to lay his head." (Matthew 8:20) Jesus had no place to call home and no synagogue or church to preach from yet it did not limit His work. When All-American athletes would attend UCLA to play basketball for John Wooden the first thing he would teach them is how to put on their socks and shoes. It is the most basic of fundamentals needed to play the game (Luther, 2010). I think sports ministries need to get back to the most basic of fundamentals in their work as well.

Mission mindset

J. Mack and Leeann Stiles created a guideline for mission work in a book titled, "Mack and Leeann's Guide to Short-Term Missions." The guideline dealt with the importance of missions taking place where a certain location has no structure to hold worship services. I believe a sports ministry without a facility is in the same shape as a group of people wishing to start a church where no building structure exists. The reference is made of Abraham pulling up his roots and going to a place where God would show him later.

"Missions are the responsibility of every Christian" (Stiles & Stiles, 2000). During my time of leading and participating in short-term missions I learned that missionaries, when they move into a different part of the world enter that world and minister in that culture. A friend of mine took a group to South America on missions and about the fourth day of work one of his team asked, "I keep making adjustments for [everyone]. I want to know when they are going to start making adjustments for me." He obviously did not catch the understanding of the mission. I always enjoyed seeing Type-A personalities with clock-watching tendencies figure out life in third-world countries where 3:00pm means sometime before 7:00pm. The aim was not to make life easy for the team, nor to make the South Americans turn into United States citizens. That would turn the team into American Judaizes. The purpose was to share Christ in the culture and ways of that particular people group.

The aim of our sports ministry, whether we have facilities or not, is to infiltrate our culture with the message of Christ's love, forgiveness, and hope.

"Go therefore and make disciples of all nations, baptizing them in the name of the Father and of the Son and of the Holy Spirit, teaching them to observe all that I have commanded you. And behold, I am with you always, to the end of the age." (Matthew 28:19-20)
I believe this includes sports. What is the culture of an athlete? Most would say, "I just want to play!" So give them a place to play!
Blessing or burden?

Neil Cole, in his book *Organic Church: Growing Faith Where Life Happens,* points out the early church did not have any buildings for more than 300 years. He further commented that Thom Wolf, International president and professor of global studies at the University Institute in New Delhi, India, actually instructs church planters to have a three-hundred-year old building plan as a part of their church planting strategy (Cole, 2005).

Rick Warren, pastor of Saddleback Church in southern California, waited fifteen years before this church bought land and constructed a facility. He reminds people of Winston Churchill's quote, "We shape our buildings and then our buildings shape us" (Warren, 1995). The same shaping takes place when we construct sports and recreation facilities in our churches. We often limit ourselves with a lack of vision in how God might bless the growth of our ministries. This shapes future opportunities of witnessing through sports.

Caz McCaslin, founder of Upward Sports, tells the story of his ministry's beginning by sharing that he was trying to fit too many children into a basketball league using one gym. He was able to recruit enough funds from a friend in the church to expand a youth facility into a basketball court for that season. He knew the next year he would need more space. The next year he approached the same man, but was told "You don't need another gym… What you need is one thousand gyms." McCaslin realized to "build" more gyms meant sharing the concept of the evangelistic league with other churches (History, 2016). Upward leagues all over the country are now being conducted despite a church not owning their own facility or field to host the league.

Cole reminds us of four different times in the Bible the Scriptures plainly state God does not dwell in buildings made by human hands (Cole, 2005). I'll refer to two of the references. When the temple was dedicated by Solomon he said, "But will God indeed dwell on the earth? Behold, heaven and the highest heaven cannot contain you; how much less this house that I have built!" (1 Kings 8:27) Stephen, prior to his martyred death makes the same claim in saying, "Yet the Most High does not dwell in houses made by hands, as the prophet says." (Acts 7:48)

A ministry can be built without the ownership of a facility or a field. God's provision does not always include a building program nor does a ministry exist simply by building a field complex or a sport facility. A facility is not a ministry until ministry occurs in the facility. In fact, in many churches, good facilities can become an idol for the church membership. I worked at two churches where the policies of usage for the facility were changed from members only plus up to two guests; to an open door policy where the entire community was invited to use the place. Battles and discussions ensued from those who felt ownership of the facility because their tithes and offerings were paying for the facility. Those wishing to keep it controlled wanted it to remain looking new rather than looking used. The concern was for how the facility looked rather than how effective it was at reaching a community. Even if a church or ministry owns facilities and fields, the mission outlook should motivate them to go out to the people rather than always trying to get the people to come to them.

What is that in your hand?

Moses had been given a great command by God to deliver the children of Israel away from slavery and bondage by the Egyptians. Doubt entered the mind of Moses as to whether Pharaoh would believe God sent him. So "the Lord said to him [Moses], "What is that in your hand?" He said, "A staff." (Exodus 4:2) The very staff Moses held was the tool God used to deliver His children from Egypt. Later, David slew a great giant with something he carried around with him while watching sheep. A simple sling slew Goliath and led to his being King as recorded in 1 Samuel 17. "And he found a fresh jawbone of a donkey, and put out his hand and took it, and with it he struck 1,000 men." (Judges 15:15) A need arose to feed a lot of people after Jesus had spoken to the crowd. Andrew found a boy with five barley loaves and two small fish. He gave them to Jesus with a stated doubt as to what good so little could do. Jesus proceeded to feed the large crowd with what they had available and ended up with twelve baskets of leftovers as recorded in John 6.

Finding a place to host sports leagues and tournaments is not difficult. One simply has to look for what is already available. Two different mission experiences in Brazil found us playing soccer on vacant lots in neighborhoods. The draw of sports gathered the crowd

Bach (1993) suggests three prerequisites before determining informal sport facilities (p. 285):

that later heard a gospel invitation. In the Dominican Republic a playground was used to instruct children as to the fundamentals of volleyball. More than just a volleyball net was cast that week as many children heard of Jesus for the first time. In the Tilbury section of London, a large meeting room and a Leisure Centre was used to teach basketball and share Christ. The Leisure Centre had a gym that was set up for badminton as no one ever played basketball. We converted the court for basketball as well for a group of children that week.

Temporal accessibility: The site or space must be available for the use of citizens at reasonable times, such as afternoon or early evening hours.

When Jesus sent his disciples to cast out demons and heal the sick He told them to bring nothing for the journey, and he called the twelve together and gave them power and authority over all demons and to cure diseases, and he sent them out to proclaim the kingdom of God and to heal. And he said to them, "Take nothing for your journey, no staff, nor bag, nor bread, nor money; and do not have two tunics. And whatever house you enter, stay there, and from there depart. And wherever they do not receive you, when you leave that town shake off the dust from your feet as a testimony against them." And they departed and went through the villages, preaching the gospel and healing everywhere. (Luke 9:1-6) The message is clear here…What you have is not as important as what you can tell.

Spatial accessibility: The site or space must be physically accessible at all times, i.e., it should not be completely fenced in or locked.

Possible resources

With some creative out of the box thinking a sports ministry leader can find is a place to conduct just about any sport without a traditional venue. Options include vacant lots, parking lots, hiking trails, and large yards or open spaces. Bach (1993) refers to this as "quantitative space" (p. 285), which is defined as available space allocated for use when the primary user does not need to use the area or parts of it full-time or part of the time. Bach (1993) further discusses space in a ***temporal, spatial, and consent for use*** capacity. It is also possible to play one sport on the court/field of another sport. For example, one can move a portable basketball goal onto a tennis court and have a makeshift basketball court.

Consent for use: The shared use of a site or space for informal sports activities must be consented to or permitted by its owner or legal tenant.

Erma Bombeck, in her short story The Coach Who Played to Lose, tells of a man that put together his own baseball league. He grew tired of seeing children at the end of a bench that never got to play in a game and began his own game. They played in an old farm field using a car seat for first, a wadded up jacket for second, and noticed an object was already available for third base. When a new player pointed out third base was cow dung, he said, "Don't slide" (Martens, 1978). A determined leader will find a place to conduct a sports league or tournament.

The ***use of facilities*** from other organizations or agencies is another option for hosting the league or tournament. "Shared use, also termed joint use, refers to the sharing of a facility by two or more organizations" (Kanters et al., 2014, p. 544). Please note, due to constraints such as ***liability***, operating expenses, and facility maintenance, many places will not share their facilities (Evenson & McGinn, 2004). Lee, Burgeson, Fulton and Spain (2007) reported only 59.6% of public schools surveyed nationally made their facilities available after hours. Another study demonstrated only 69% of schools allowed shared use (Spengler, Young & Linton, 2007).

Use of a facility holds many concerns such as liability. This is an obligation to do or refrain from doing something or where a duty must be performed including responsibilities for one's conduct (such as utilizing a facility whether it is the church's facility or someone else's facility.

Check with the local school system about the policies and requirements of using gym or field spaces. Local recreation or park departments also are a good place to check. Other churches in your area might have spaces as well that you can borrow or lease. Beyond leasing or borrowing, a church could also get involved in trading spaces. For example, the use of a large auditorium for graduations could be "traded" for use of the school's sports facilities.

Look into obtaining a certificate of insurance from your insurance agent, which will give you more credibility in obtaining borrowed or leased spaces. Kanters et al. (2014) discovered almost 89% of North Carolina schools allowed for shared use. His study arrived at the following conclusion of their research with North Carolina schools that allowed for shared use.

Community organizations seeking to use indoor school facilities or athletic fields should be prepared to complete a formal written use agreement. However, access to playgrounds and running tracks may be achieved with little to no formality. A school history of low or no shared use may not be an indication of a school's unwillingness to allow community use of their facilities (Kanters et al., 2014). This kind of ***planning*** for shared facilities may require some creativity as your need for the gym or baseball field may have to be arranged during their off season planning.

Planning involves setting goals for your sports ministry and the stakeholders involved with the program by specifying activities to achieve such goals. "Without planning, managers wouldn't know what to organize, lead, or control." (Robbins, Coulter & Langton, 2006, p. 160)

Beyond the box

If the opportunity to reach people is available, a sports minister might need to think outside the box in order to provide the facilities to host a league, tournament, or event. Some churches are establishing training programs for coaches. Once trained these men and women volunteer to coach in existing leagues offered by YMCA's or city recreation departments. It is a different way to present the gospel in sports ministry. Some churches place teams of their own in other leagues hoping to use that as a witness. One must be careful to train the team on how to be missionaries in a city league. Far too often the church has the opposite effect.

A church might have to operate sports outside their traditional time frame. If weather allows a field for soccer or baseball can be found in the off-season part of the year. There is no reason basketball has to be a fall and early spring sport. Portable equipment can also be rented and parking lot tournaments can be held. Many communities hire out 3 on 3 basketball tournament formats that are conducted in such a fashion.

Finally, a Mobile Recreation Van or Trailer can be made. This idea is used by several city recreation departments in making space and equipment available to different parts of their community. A hinged basketball goal is attached to the back of the van and equipment such as balls, cones, and flags are contained inside the van. No need for a fancy facility when you have one on wheels. The need for spaces, fields, and facilities are only as limited as the creativity of the leader. The opportunities are endless if one is determined enough to make the ministry possible.

Learning-to-action exercise

Tour your church, list three (3) areas could you conduct activities for your sports ministry? What type of activities could take place in those spaces?

1. ____

a. Activity____

2. ____

a. Activity____

3. ____

a. Activity____

Who would you speak with at your church, to see the opportunities available to hold one or more activities in these spaces?

____

____

Look in your local phone and find three (3) resources such as Yelp or Yellow Pages and list the possible resources available for use or adaptive use of your sports ministry.

1. ____

a. Contact information______________________________

2. ____

b. Contact information______________________________

4. ____

c. Contact information______________________________

Use the space below to write out steps (or develop a plan) to organize and utilize the information above that you have collected to benefit your sports ministry program.

CHAPTER NINE

CONFLICT MANAGEMENT

within Sports Ministry

"It's not if it happens, but when it happens..."

Greg English - Recreation Minister
Cool Spring Baptist Church, Mechanicsville, VA
@recreatn
CSRM Board of Trustee Chair
Adjunct Professor - Chowan University

The season started with great enthusiasm. Several hundred players signed up, coaches accepted the opportunity to invest both spiritually and physically into the players, and parents were excited to have their child participating in a league that offers sport and character development.

From the perspective of a recreation minister or director, all looked bright. Besides, with the emphasis of spiritual growth why would you anticipate anything other than a great peaceful season?

Then it happened. After weeks of practice and after the first game, the breakdown occurred. Two coaches that had not met before agreed to work together for a positive purpose—to introduce spiritual disciplines and develop specific sport skills. The assigned head coach was having difficulty with a particular player, the assistant coach's child. Trying a variety of approaches first, he then reached out to the league director for help. Unfortunately, his frustration level clouded his mind and rather than emailing his complaints about the child to the league director, the email was accidentally sent to the father of the child. Thereby creating the conflict that would quickly unfold. Once the email was received by the other coach and father of the child, a quick tempered response was sent back to the head coach on his inappropriate actions and his lack of knowledge on how to even coach and work with children. As you can imagine, this quickly ran itself out of control as a result of the email chains that circled back and forth.

In order to address the issue as fast as possible, the league director and recreation minister contacted both parties and called for a meeting. The goal was to diffuse the situation and seek reconciliation. The leadership understood that through emails going back and forth, much confusion and unkind slurs were not the way to deal with the conflict appropriately. The meeting was established with the goal of reconciliation. The reconciliation could mean that both parties apologize and work through better strategies or that either coach could be removed for the purpose of creating the best sports experience possible for the team. Fortunately, after the discussion and addressing the apologies and ways to better handle player issues, both coaches resolved their efforts and were able to finish the season in a positive manner.

If there is one thing I have learned over the years, it is that you cannot wish away conflict from the arena of sports, even in a league that desires Christian principles. Conflict will happen and what you do with it will determine the results of the league and development of the players, coaches, and families involved. Conflict can be described as a struggle or clash between opposing forces; a state of opposition between ideas, interests, etc., disagreement or controversy between people whether caused by the differences in behaviors, decisions, interests, or desires of outcomes. Within sports, conflict is often perceived as negative. This negative response is a by-product of stressful moments, anxiety, unresolved relationship issues between participants and specific situations. However, conflict does not have to be a negative. In fact, conflict can produce positive outcomes in the individual and sport experience. When appropriately dealt with in a timely manner conflict actually produces growth and change. Here are ways in which conflict affects both negatively and positively:

Negative Outcomes	Positive Outcomes
People feel defeated, anxious, and stressed	Motivation and creativity occur as a result of seeking new approaches
A distrustful environment is created	Clarification and communication of ideas
Lack of Communication	Trust increases and team performance improves
Poor team relationships	The sport experience for all participating creates a desire for continued participation and positive feedback
Productivity of successful experience declines	Accountability becomes a high mark for league reputation

Once conflict is viewed as positive, the commitment to relationships and development increases. Conflict is not the preferred way people want to experience personal growth. In fact, most people want to avoid conflict. But conflict generates growth and is very effective in life learning for all.

Conflict can occur in many areas of the sport and recreation ministry program. Whether you are responsible for the programming of a recreation and fitness center, adult and youth leagues, or coach and player development programs, conflict can easily find its way in. Why? Because at the core of who we are as individuals desires an expected performance level or result that benefits the me over others. It is the desire for self-gratification in certain areas of our lives over the glory of God in all things we do (see 1 Corinthians 10:31). Additional conflict may arise due to the desire to relive an experience that was not achieved previously as players or participants. The second chance opportunity to prove worth through a sports experience often overshadows the end results of development for players and coaches. Conflict also occurs because of misunderstandings of expectations or interpretations of guidelines and rules between two parties. Most times it is not a people problem but a situation problem that causes conflict. While people are involved and actions can be distracting or contradictory to the purpose of the program, the conflict originates as a result of a specific situation in the gym, on the field, or in the game. Remember the story of the two coaches. It was not necessarily the coach that was the problem. It was a result of the situation in which he addressed it that caused the conflict. Conflicts in sports occur frequently as a result of the pressures of competition. Conflicts will arise before, during, or after the competition when the participants are most stressed and the amplified feeling of winning or losing is expressed with those desires. Whether you are a coach, athlete, or sports parent, you will need to understand the best way to recognize and manage conflict in a way that results in a positive outcome.

The Thomas-Kilmann Conflict Mode is a tool for helping people understand how different conflict-handling styles affect interpersonal and group dynamics.

The Thomas-Kilmann Conflict Mode Instrument identifies areas in which people deal with conflict and assess an individual's behavior in conflict situations. Within conflict, both assertiveness, extent to which the individual attempts to satisfy his or her own concerns, and cooperativeness, extent to which the individual attempts to satisfy the others person's concerns, are observed. There are five areas that the Thomas-Kilmann Conflict Mode Instrument points out as ways people respond to conflict.

COMPETING:

Living in a mindset of competition creates a struggle for power. Typically, the individual will be uncooperative and seek his or her own gain at the expense of others. This action often hurts others in the process.

COLLABORATING:

The action of collaboration allows for a "team" approach. It involves individuals who are seeking to understand the perspectives of others, while creating a solution that will benefit both. Though the initial process can be a result of disagreement or division, there is the desire to make things right. This approach is assertive and cooperative.

COMPROMISING:

The individual desires to find a resolution to satisfy both parties. It seeks to see at what levels are their similarities and address them for a solution. The comprising objective takes the "middle ground" approach so that conflict can be avoided.

To avoid means to allow. Any conflict that is not addressed continues to build. While some prefer to avoid or postpone an issue, withdrawing from the conflict will not create resolution. You will hear people say, "let's ignore it or we need to wait for another time to handle it."

AVOIDING:

To avoid means to allow. Any conflict that is not addressed continues to build. While some prefer to avoid or postpone an issue, withdrawing from the conflict will not create resolution. You will hear people say, "let's ignore it or we need to wait for another time to handle it."

ACCOMMODATING:

The individual causes self-sacrifice in order to remove the conflict. The concerns of others involved outweigh the concern of the individual. Often these people are "people pleasers" want the problem to be resolved, even if it causes them sacrifice.

[13] This instrument is derived from the following reference. Thomas, Kenneth W. and Kilmann, Ralph H. Thomas-Kilmann Conflict Mode Instrument: A Profile and Interpretive Report. March 2010. The key words are the same words from the instrument, however the descriptions are written to fit the context of sports ministry.

As a recreation minister or recreation director within the local church, as well as other areas of life, it will serve you well to understand the levels of the conflict modes used by Thomas-Kilmann assessment. By using these five areas, the sports ministry professional will be able to identify early behaviors of particular people involved in and assisting in reaching the overall goal of the ministry. By discerning these responses, conflict can be kept to a minimum and addressed in proper timing (Thomas & Kilmann, 2010). In fact, many can already identify specific people's actions concerning conflict. One way to assist in helping you create the best experience possible, think about those individuals and the positions they serve in. How can you work with them early so that growth occurs rather than in the midst of conflict?

Managing conflict among participants

Culture can be seen as an ambiguous term as there are so many cultures we are accustomed. Culture is constantly evolving. For example, college freshman today are seen differently than college freshmen 30 years ago. This is why we often see conflict within sport...conflict/cultural theorists suggest that conflict often arises due to different (sport) cultural upbringings in additional to other societal factors such as socio-economic and educational. To manage conflict, understanding cultural backgrounds may smooth the way for conflict mediation.

The sports ***culture*** finds conflict in a variety of relationships. The relationships involve coach and player, coach and referee, coach and parent, player and referee, parent and coach, parent and referee, and parent and player. While observing or watching sports programs, make note of all that is happening with the activity between each party. One of the things I have done over the years through my sons' participation in athletics has been observation. In fact, I consider myself a researcher of people groups in the sports arena (a sociologist if you will). Traveling from location to location and tournament to tournament in a variety of places around the east coast, I have found my share of stories to reflect on and learn from, both positive and negative. From the time that two parents fought in the bleachers over one child's behavior toward the other child's to a coach graciously acknowledging the winning team's character and actions on the floor. Conflict is present and it is sad we do not have to look far to observe it.

Coach to player / Coach to referee

The role of a coach, outside of the parent, may be the best investment young people receive. But the role of a coach with a degrading culture can also be the worst investment a child can experience. Conflict among the two can be caused for a variety of reasons: playing time, attitude regarding play formations, treatment towards others, and philosophy. Unfortunately, not dealing with these issues early with an open culture of communication will create frustration and wound a relationship. Recently, I had the opportunity to coach a middle school age soccer team. After winning several games and making adjustments in the lineup that allowed for these players to experience a variety of positions, one of our team members was visibly upset after a great comeback win. Taking note of the situation, I spoke with him on the sideline. Because we had established a culture of communication, he told me he was disappointed he did not play defense during the game. This conversation opened my eyes. It first gave me a sense of joy that we had a culture to fend off conflict by communication and it helps me understand his perspective. He did not complain he was on the offensive side, but he did express his desire to play defense because that was his area of interest. Yes, there are many scenarios that go into making team position decisions, but also on this day, not only did we deal with the potential conflict, but we also created a positive ending to the would be conflict if not addressed.

One of the areas of conflict that presents a larger problem is with the coaches' relationship to the referees. While most coaches preach the proper attitude of sportsmanship, they seldom live it out on the sideline. Listening in on a practice or pre-game speech will make you think the coach has the correct perspective. Then the ball is put in play and another person shows up. The actions of a coach are powerful and the actions of the coach are reproducible in children and teams. When the coach finds fault with every call the referee makes and decides to verbally abuse the referee or dehumanize the person, you can be sure the team will follow. Rather than making adjustments as a coach, the stress level creates more frustration on and off the bench. Observing a tournament basketball game one Saturday, I was able to see first-hand this scenario play out. The coach, claiming his innocence and proper demeanor, berated the officials up and down the court. Never was it his fault as a coach why the press was not being broken or the child could not make an inside move, but rather it was the referee's fault. What followed would be the constant questioning of the referee and eventually those working the scorer's table. In order to restore the game experience, a technical foul was called. The frustration level by now moved from coach to the players. Players were now questioning the authority of every call and throwing water bottles on the bench. Conflict ensued and league directors had to step in and address the coach at halftime. Shocked by the corrections provided by the league, the coach then created greater conflict that day. What occurred that day could have been stopped at the beginning of the conflict if the coach would have spoken directly in a professional manner with the referee to gain a better understanding of the reason for the calls being made. Proper communication and perspective could have created a better experience for all.

Parent to coach / League to coach and parent

Every parent believes the best of their child. And in today's culture, many parent believes his or her child will be the one to make it professionally. If only they would read and understand that statistics show otherwise. Conflict among parents and coaches occurs on every level, from recreation to travel teams, school sports, and college. Parents feeling as though their child is not receiving the proper amount of playing time or being treated unfairly compared to others on the team. In order to remove these conflicts, coaches and parents must meet and establish the goals of the team. Whether that is skill sets or playing opportunities, without understanding upfront of what both parent and their child can expect, conflict can occur. The proactive approach to communication regarding expectations will open dialogue throughout the season that will provide a positive sports experience.

The same is true for league directors or sports administrators in relationship to the coaches and parents involved. Having the proper

[14] According to a 2016 study done by the National Collegiate Athletic Association (NCAA), of the 480,000 that compete in the NCAA only a select few from several sports that have professional leagues make it. Baseball (9.7%), Men's Ice Hockey (6.6%), Football (1.6%), Men's Soccer (1.4%), Men's Basketball (1.1%), and Women's Basketball (0.9%)

understanding of the purpose of the league (recreation or travel team) has to be established early. In many cases, those participating have a different view of how the sport should be played or participated in. When offering a recreation league, the points of development and the experience of fun have to be communicated. If it is a travel team, the purpose, development and winning tournaments, also has to be discussed. When an unspoken position is taken and parents have paid fees or travel expenses, conflict will arise and criticism of the league or coach will take place. Remember, every parent has dreams and desires for their child. When those dreams do not appear to becoming true, self-interests typically take over and create unnecessary conflict. To avoid these situations, recreation ministers and directors need to know the purpose of the programming they are offering and ensuring that those involved know the same reasons for the sports experience. In order to help prevent conflict in these areas, write down each league or team sport offered. Then write down its purpose for development both physically and spiritually. One is not better than the other, but if you do not have clear communication of goals and positions, you can be sure you will be having conversations of conflict.

Parent to player

One of the most disappointing conflicts occurring in sports today is the relationship between the parent and the player. Most of these conflicts occur because the parent does not understand the desire of the child and child does not understand the desire of the parent. What may be innocent participation in the beginning of a child's playing career can turn into a situation in which neither party is experiencing the enjoyment of the sport because of unrealistic expectations. Returning to the gym in which I have had the pleasure to watch my sons play sports, I witnessed one of the saddest stories in my years of sports ministry and management. Each week I would go to the local community basketball league to watch my son play on Saturday. It was nice for me to go and watch him play in another league where I was not the recreation director. It was refreshing to just be his father and cheer him on in his endeavors. Unfortunately, what I began to observe of another father was the overwhelming stress on him to produce the best basketball player in the league. The father would never sit in the stands to watch with the others. He positioned himself in the corners of the gym depending on which side his son's team was playing offense. It was there that he constantly barked out orders against the coach and instructed his son to do better. Whatever the child did, dribble, shoot, pass, it was never good enough. This took place week after week. Finally, the conflict blew up. On one particular game towards the end of the season, the son missed a shot. The father then expressed his disappointment in how he missed such a shot. While running up the court to return to play defense, the child turned and screamed at his father in a loud gruff voice "shut-up." The whole gym fell in silence and sorrow for both the child and father. It was apparent that the father had dreams and visions, which the child did not at that time. He simply wanted to enjoy playing with his friends in a local youth program. As result, the parent was asked not to attend the games unless another parent or family member accompanied him. One of the areas in which the recreation minister or director can aid in is helping parents create realistic expectations for their children through sports. Not only is it important to speak into the lives of coaches and players in the league, but also the need to speak into the lives of parents has become greater. Unrealistic expectations and conflict within the early years of a child's sports experience can create long-term relationship problems between families.

Spectators to referees

Everyone loves to "booo" a referee and tell them how bad they are. It is as if our sports culture accepts this as normal. Sure, this has been around for years, but the intensity is rising. I am amazed of the number of times that I have spoken to spectators during games regarding behavior to see them do the complete opposite five minutes later. The level of stress a competitive experience can create can be surprising, but also expected. Remember, it is through these circumstances that people's lack of self-control comes out leaving the recreation minister or director the responsibility to deal with the conflict. One of more shocking situations occurred between a father of a fifth grader and his friend who was refereeing a youth game. These gentlemen see each other weekly and speak regularly. However, this event, a tournament game, produced an unfriendly altercation. With the game being played at a high level, as high a level as a fifth grade game can be played, what was thought to be travel by the father was not called by his friend. What ensued next was really unbelievable. The father proceeded to stand up in the bleachers amongst everyone and yell, "traveling" with the hand gestures of the travel call. Committed to not giving up on making sure his referee friend saw his interpretation of what should have been called and telling him how bad he missed it, the referee simply responded by not responding, a good decision in the midst of the game. Following the game, another friend in the stands approached the father to correct him and hold him accountable for his actions towards the referee. It was a teachable moment that needed to happen. Too often, spectators have to be addressed for inappropriate actions that cause conflict among others in the stands, community leaders, and participants in the games.

With conflict occurring in our sports culture, how should you really respond? Do you simply work towards behavior management or seek transformation in the lives of those participating? I suggest transformation. Many hours can be spent on behavior management causing frustration for the recreation minister or director of the local church. Yet when we put into place a culture that introduces and teaches transformation from a biblical perspective, we see results of individuals seeing themselves for who they are and who they can become according to God's plan and glory.

The Bible speaks of conflict. In fact, conflict scenarios are not unbiblical when handled correctly. They are part of life and Jesus himself speaks to conflict resolution and reconciliation between individuals. Remember the goal of conflict is reconciliation and can result in positive growth outcomes. Matthew 18:16 and 5:23-26 provide clear directions for resolution.

"If your brother sins against you, go and tell him his fault, between you and him alone. If he listens to you, you have gained your brother. But if he does not listen, take one or two others along with you, that the evidence of two or three witnesses may establish every charge. If he refuses to listen to them, they'll the church. And if he refuses to listen even to the church, let him be as to you as a Gentile and a tax collector." (Matthew 18:15-17)

"So if you are offended your gift at the altar and there are members that your brother has something against you, leave your gift there before the altar and go. First be reconciled to your brother, and then come offer your gift. Come to terms quickly with your accuser while you are going with him to court, lest your accuser hand you over to the judge, and the judge to the guard, and you be put in prison." (Matthew 5:23-25)

These passages of scripture speak to the reconciliation process. Reconciliation is about restoration and putting back in place. With the multitudes of competitive energies in today's sports arenas, it is easy for relationships to be disrupted through conflict. What we learn from these passages in regard to conflict and relationships is that it costs less to address the root of a conflict early on than to carry the weight of the consequences of the conflict fully developed. The earlier the conflict is addressed and managed correctly, the less the effects of avoidance occur. If you look to the prior passages found in Matthew 18:10-14 we actually see the concept of God pursuing his people, even just one person. Just as God pursues the one who strays, so should we pursue reconciliation in relationships and conflicts that occur in the sports culture. Again, in the following verses 21-35 we see the concept of forgiveness being taught. The forgiveness of God is so great towards us that a payback is not required. As we follow Christ, it should reflect the same attitude of forgiveness towards those we find ourselves in conflict with. The key word in conflict reconciliation is forgiveness. Forgiveness allows the actions of a recreation minister or director, coach, player, parent, or ref to pursue the one in conflict, be willing to forgive, and seek to restore what's been broken in the relationship.

When managing conflict from a biblical perspective, here are few practical reminders to pursue:

Practice emotional intelligence – Jesus had a way of reading the emotional level of individuals and crowds. Be wise in your understanding of what may be causing particular actions or outcries of individuals. Often times I have found that it had nothing to do with the game or other team, but the fact the individual was having specific struggles in his or her life and they needed grace and patience.

Everything begins with a conversation – Having the one-on-one conversation increases the likelihood of that the confrontation or conflict is being addressed in a genuine manner. A one-on-one conversation also addresses the issue privately rather than a public berating or gossip of the other person involved. Finally, it demonstrates the desire for reconciliation and creates the likelihood assuming the best results.

Articulate your thoughts – Knowing the approach and the way in which you desire to restore the relationship will enable you to avoid the abuse of tearing down the person and rather addressing the issue. Ephesians 4:15, "Rather speaking the truth in love…" When we express grace to those in the midst of conflict, we find that the return is also given to those addressing the conflict and the pursuit of reconciliation can occur in a timely manner.

Listen well to each other – Be willing to hear the heart of the person speaking without taking their response personally. As a recreation minister or director, you have to establish the ability to listen well and avoid taking issues personally. Sure, owning certain situations is part of leadership, but there are times that listening well simply means hearing their perspectives. Focus on the person and acknowledge their concerns and recognize they have something they need or want to express, validate them. Other ways include asking questions and restating the concerns they have shared.

Demonstrate a sense of self-control – In the middle of conflict, particularly a competitive event, the outcome desired may not occur or even be heard by others. During these times self-control must be displayed and the next step in reconciliation involving others needs to occur. It is much easier to loose self-control and express how you see the situation and feel about it, but the leader within you must demonstrate self-control and prepare for the next steps. Addressing the problem rather than the emotions enables clear decision making processes.

Pray through the process – Praying for the individual(s) involved in the conflict allows for the leader to love them in process. It also creates a care and concern for them that only God can instill. Work for the Win!—This does not mean that as a leader you get the outcome you want or everything you demand to see will happen. It means, "You have gained your brother." That's the win! A reconciled relationship and resolved conflict that ultimately brings honor to God and the people involved.

Managing conflict within your sport and recreation ministry is about having right relationships. Relationships that include other league directors, coaches, families, and players. When these relationships begin to be strained for one reason or another, research why, meet with the people involved, seek forgiveness, and create a win for everyone.

Communication shows the act or process of using words, sounds, signs, or behaviors to express or exchange information or to express your ideas, thoughts, feelings, etc., to someone else. Communication involves both sending and receiving information, verbal and nonverbal forms, and can occur one-on-one or within group settings. (Pedersen & Thibault, 2014)

What communication means for participants

The life of a sport administrator, league director, or coach evolves around healthy *communication*. What we learn from conflict management is that a majority of issues are results of bad communication processes. Therefore, addressing communication must be included in conflict management processes.

Administrators and coaches alike will participate in numerous avenues of communication each season; from parent and player emails to team discussions after practices or games. It is understood that the success of the program, coach experience, and parental expectations all depend on good communication. Unfortunately, we have all made that comment that we regret and have failed to communicate the vision of the program or team. It was not long ago I was having breakfast with a coach from our youth league. A veteran coach of three years who I would have thought he knew the mission and purpose for what the league wanted to accomplish, until a specific scenario arose. It was during this conversation that I heard him say, "I don't know what the league wants to accomplish or how its states its purpose." Needless to say, not only was that a reflection of the league (which hurts branding...see Chapter 7) but it was a reflection of me as a sport administrator. I realized then that poor communication of mission and purpose to our coaches led to a conflict situation that could have been avoided.

Note that non-verbal communication is primary source to deliver any message. Dr. Albert Mehrabian, author of Silent Messages, conducted several studies on nonverbal communication. He found that 7% of any message is conveyed through words, 38% through certain vocal elements, and 55% through nonverbal elements (facial expressions, gestures, posture, etc.). Subtracting the 7% for actual vocal content leaves one with the 93% statistic.

Becoming an effective communicator is not easy. It takes thought, intentionality, and practice. It also takes understanding the means in which best to communicate. Today's culture often uses social media and other forms of communication that can hinder the genuineness of the relationship and create habits of poor communication skills. While good communication skills will enhance the participants experience and remove the breakdowns that lead to distrust, frustration, and dissatisfaction.

As a model of good communication, we can look to the life Jesus. Jesus' demonstration of good communication was demonstrated and shared to others. In most of His conversations we find Him speaking specifically in an understandable language to the audience he was addressing. Depending on the situation, Jesus was speaking to crowds, small groups, or to individuals. He had an understanding for interpreting His message in the context to which His listeners would respond. Jesus not only verbalized his messages, but also demonstrated them with practical and life changing examples. Those watching not only heard the stories being told, but also witnessed the miracles that Jesus performed and was affirmed by James in his epistle (see James 1:19).

1. Everyone must learn to become a good listener—"Know this, my beloved brothers: let every person be quick to hear,

2. Everyone must learn to be a guided speaker—slow to speak

3. Everyone must learn to respond in gentleness—slow to anger

Conflict is inevitable…you must remember that sports ministry is about relationships and communication. Anytime you have relationships you will have communication and both can encounter conflict. In order for others to pursue reconciliation and manage conflict accordingly, the recreation minister or director and his or her staff must be willing to exhibit conflict resolution and teach the biblical model of doing so.

Conflict resolution activity

Greg English and Jenny Young have worked together over the years to develop conflict management resolution webinars and both believe that talking about conflict with those directly and indirectly related to your sports ministry will better prepare sports ministers when conflict does arise. Together, they have written a case study for you to think about and discuss with others. Prior to the case study, sport minister can prepare to manage conflict by analyzing the following objectives:

1. Identify, conduct additional research, and learn about the causes of conflict in sport situations

2. Learn how to anticipate conflict in your particular sports ministry

3. Learn how to resolve and demonstrate conflict resolution in your sports ministry

"A common place" - Conflict resolution case study

Overseeing any sports and recreation ministry can be challenging. However, when the challenge is a result of a sports and recreation ministry being devalued or not seen as effective, it makes for a difficult position to be in. Read the following true scenario:

"We cannot grow the sports ministry as space limits us on the church campus and surrounding facilities. We need to downsize the ministry in order to accommodate the school and church. This means you, the sports minister, will need to reduce participants and maybe even staff in order to manage what you have since you are a sports recreation program with people paying less to play than those who go to school paying for an excellent program."

If you have never experienced conflict, here it is. In fact, this situation opens up more than one conflict. Work through the following:

1. Determine the parties involved within the conflict. Identify their positions and reasons for them.

2. What conflict or conflicts can you identify?

3. How does a sports minister approach this scenario? Do you begin with individual conversations? Do you present the value of the recreation program to all parties involved? Do you challenge the thinking of the school or administration?

[15] Jenny Young is the Director of the Soar Sports ministry program for Christ Covenant Church in Matthews, NC

4. What is or should be the goal (outcome) of the sports minister and his or her position of ministry as it is being shared with other ministries on campus?

Additional conflict resolution topics are as follows:

1. Think about the last conflict you have been involved in (fight on the field, verbal argument in the stands, etc.) involving players, coaches, or parents. What caused the conflict? Discuss the causes and write them down.

2. Determine the reasons for the conflicts occurring. Use note-pads to write each option down that can reveal specific themes or causes. Examples could include over aggressive play, high level of competition, or poor officiating.

CHAPTER TEN

MEASURING MINISTRY EFFECTIVENESS:

Tracking & Reporting Ministry Opportunities

Dave Bundrick - Minister of Fitness and Recreation
Houston's First Baptist Church
@davebundrick
Former CSRM Board of Trustee Chair

At sixteen years of age, I felt God calling me to recreation ministry as my full-time vocation. At that time, I did not realize that such a ministry existed.

What I did know was that my small church in the suburbs of Houston had built a gym, and that gym was creating real opportunities for me to do ministry. We did not have a formal recreation ministry, but I found it much easier to invite my friends to come play basketball or pool rather than Sunday School or Worship. I enjoyed activities in the gym and found it more natural to connect with people in those environments. I experienced, first-hand, people coming to the church for the first time through our gym doors.

At the time of writing this chapter, I have spent 19 years serving in a full-time capacity as Minister of Fitness & Recreation (or some variation thereof) and am at my third local church. The first two churches I served were start-ups as I was hired to lead the creation of the sports ministry. My most recent post finds me serving in a ministry that was created about the time I felt called to ministry (three decades ago). I remain convinced that now, more than ever, when used properly, Sport, Recreation & Fitness (SRF) ministries can be used as a local church's most effective outreach tool. These ministries can naturally connect churches to their communities. The question is, if this is the case, why do we not see more local churches investing in these ministries? We have even seen churches that once believed in these ministries, abandon them. I believe part of the flaw here lies with the sports ministry manager communicating the impact that the SRF Ministry has on its participants to the leadership of the faith community (i.e., senior pastors, elders and congregation).

Early in my ministry, my pastor was very supportive of the ministry, but part of my job was to help him understand the ministry and communicate with him in such a way that he could easily share the impact of the ministry with others in the church. He wanted to do this, and he intrinsically understood the value, but he needed solid evidence and stories that affirmed the church's decision to venture into this ministry. I found that the concept of ***Ministry Opportunities*** helped track, record and, translate program activity into terms that church leaders better understood. The concept Ministry Opportunity also reinforced that a SRF Ministry is exactly that, a Ministry.

Ministry opportunities are any occasion to inspire someone to begin or build their own relationship with God.

Similar to other sport ministry programs around the country, SRF Ministries like ours in Houston, TX, are by nature, ministries of activity. I believe the staff and volunteers leading these ministries are action-oriented people. This is a great benefit but is also a great liability. We as sport ministers can get so focused working IN the ministry that we neglect to work ON the ministry. Often, sports ministries are very effective in helping the church accomplish its mission, but we sometimes we fail to communicate the impact in a manner that church leadership understands or appreciates. It is the responsibility of sport ministries to adapt their messaging to better communicate the impact of their ministry. It all starts with tracking. In order to report impact to church stakeholders, we must devise and implement methods of tracking impact. *Impact* must also be communicated to church leadership and other stakeholders in terms they are accustomed to.

The essence of **impact**, from a Ministry Opportunity perspective, is the impression left on participants as a result of having participated in an activity that otherwise would not be impacted.

There are two basic categories of data to be tracked and reported for a sports ministry: Quantitative and Qualitative. Quantitative data can be counted and calculated. Common methods of collecting quantitative data are: Surveys, registrations, attendance numbers, financial reports, etc. Qualitative data comes in the form of stories and testimonies. Common methods of collecting qualitative data are: Focus groups, interviews, analysis of documents, requests for testimonies, town hall meetings, conversations, etc. Both qualitative and quantitative data have immense value. Both are necessary to paint a picture of ministry impact. To be clear, we will never fully understand the impact of these ministries this side of Heaven. I also agree with the famous sociologist William Bruce Cameron when he said, "Not everything that counts can be counted and not everything that can be counted counts." In ministry, never has this saying been truer. However, this does not mean that we should not make an effort at counting and measuring in an attempt to better understanding the impact of our ministries and the needs of those we seek to serve.

The Bible has numerous quantitative and qualitative data, divinely inspired, meticulously collected and passionately preserved. God works through this data to communicate the larger story of his love for all of mankind. Even Jesus uses quantitative and qualitative data in His teachings. Sometimes he communicates in qualitative parables and miracles. Other times, His parables and miracles are numerical in nature (the feeding of 5,000, the Parable of the Talents, etc.). The Gospel writer John records Jesus' miracle of the caught fish. (John 21:1-11) It is reported that "153 great fish" were caught. Obviously, someone took the time to count (track) and report this figure. By reporting an exact number, this shows that the details matter. In this story, the writer did not report "150 fish" or "nearly

200 fish." Exactly, "153 great fish" were caught. Both quantitative and qualitative data are reported to convey a miraculous work of God. It is important not to use this data to inflate oneself or a specific program. Rather, it should be used to provide a glimpse of God's work. We know that numbers do not bind God. For instance, consider the story of Gideon. In this famous passage, God showed His might by reducing the numbers involved. The numbers that are tracked and reported should re-emphasize God's glory and sovereignty in a converse manner.

Now that we understand the need to Track and Report both Qualitative and Quantitative data, I would like to introduce a term that better communicates ministry impact.

Ministry Opportunities

I recommend communicating the impact of your sports ministry in terms of "Ministry Opportunities." I define a Ministry Opportunity as any instance where there is an occasion to encourage someone to move closer to God. Not all Ministry Opportunities are the same, yet all are valuable. Some Ministry Opportunities will be more overtly evangelical while other opportunities may focus on establishing and growing relationships. Some programs are designed to lead people to a moment where they make a choice to accept Jesus as their savior. Others are designed to provide unintimidating, safe environments for participants.

Ministry Opportunities can be as subtle as providing a clean, welcoming environment that communicates we are excited about individuals actively (and sometimes not actively) participating. Again, I feel that every time someone leaves a ministry program, their perception of it has either increased or decreased, either way, I consider this a positive ministry opportunity. I believe that God often uses these perceptions of their experiences (both positive or negative) to draw people to Him.

I encourage you to begin thinking and communicating using the term Ministry Opportunities. Do not simply talk about how many players were in a league, use the term Ministry Opportunity to more fully communicate the impact of a program. Below is a short case study that I hope will aid in your understanding and eventual practice of the Ministry Opportunities concept:

Let's use the example of 200 children in a 10-week basketball league. I have kept it simple and say they practice one-night a week and play games on Saturdays.

- ***200 children in a league***
- ***Game days (8)***
- ***x 3 because others come to watch (Parents, siblings, grandparents, friends).***

In my experience, three (3) are a conservative multiplier for youth sports game days. Three (3) represents the player and two additional people. There is no perfect number, but I feel this number most accurately reflects the average.

- ***200 players' x 8 game days x 3 (multiplier) = 4,800 Ministry Opportunities***
- ***Practices (10)***
- ***x 2 because someone brings them to practices***
- ***200 players' x 2 (multiplier) =4,000 Ministry Opportunities***
- ***8,800 total Ministry Opportunities***

Following this formula, we can conservatively calculate that a youth sports league with 200 players generates 8,800 Ministry Opportunities over a 10-week period. I believe using this term and this formula more effectively communicates the amount of impact the league has in the community the church is serving.

It is important to not inflate the numbers. In fact, it is better to underestimate. If you lose trust in your tracking and report methods,

Credibility refers to leaders that are trustworthy, honest, competent and inspiring (Scott, 2014). According to Kouzes and Posner (2007) "Credibility is the foundation of leadership" (p. 37). Being credible is most important, especially if your ministry is just starting out.

you will lose ***credibility*** and holding credibility is everything for a sports ministry program.

Let's dive a bit further into the details of WHAT to track and report. This will vary depending on the context of your ministry and what values are upheld. It is important for you, as the leader of this ministry, to understand what is important to the organization you serve, its key stakeholders and decision makers. It is always good to collect more data than you may think you need. You may not report on all of the data you have collected, but it will be good to have it in case you want to dive a bit deeper.

Several quantitative measures I suggest are: 1) Ministry Opportunities, 2) Church affiliation, 3) Financials, 4) Interest in your church, 5) Interest or growth in their relationship with God (for participant and other family members).

I track quantitative data in weekly increments and use a spreadsheet to do so. It is a bit of work to create the system. However, once you have it established, you will find that it may take less than an hour a week to update your records. I recommend maintaining your data on a weekly basis. If you let much time lapse, it ends up being quite a bit of work to go back and input the figures. You also run the risk of your data becoming less accurate because you cannot remember specifics and have to make some assumptions. So, find time in your week for that hour (say Mondays) and be consistent, book it in your calendar as a reoccurring event to track your ministry.

To gather qualitative data, ask for stories of impact. Ask how this program benefitted the participant and his/her family. This handbook has numerous stories of impact (see Tinsley Jones—Chapter 5 stories of impact). Often, the bottom line is that we want to know if this program encouraged them spiritually and if they are interested in connecting to your particular church. Whatever you would like to know, do not hesitate to ask it. Toward the end of my program surveys, I ask if the person taking the survey could provide a sentence or two of how this program has impacted their relationship with God. You would be surprised at the openness of some respondents.

Collecting data is important to not only put a great deal of thought into when and how best to report the data, but it also can help tell the full story of the impact of your ministry. Again, it is important for you, the leader of this ministry, to understand your church's culture and the mindset of leadership. I have found that quantitative data helps with strategic program planning while qualitative data is inspiring and motivating.

The frequency of reporting will vary greatly from church to church. In all three of the churches I have served, the frequency of reporting has differed. Consider these natural opportunities to report your findings: 1) Annual church reports, 2) Deacon/Elder meetings, 3) Church business meetings, 4) All-staff meetings, 5) Strategic planning meetings, 6) Vision casting meetings, etc. Often, you will need to seek out your pastor or direct supervisor's input and permission as to when to report your findings.

In my own experience, I have found it helpful to over communicate in the beginning of my ministry at each of my churches. This helped my supervisor and the church to better understand my ministry and set realistic expectations for it. As time went on, there was less of a need to report as frequently because trust had been established, understanding of the ministry had grown and support for it had been shown. In my current context of ministry, I began by reporting monthly to my Executive Pastor. He then chose when to share those reports with the Senior Pastor and church leadership. Six years later, I prepare a report twice a year for my Executive Pastor. From time to time, my supervisor and/or church leadership will ask for a specific report. It is nice to have the data readily available so that I can report back in a timely manner. This organization is critical and helps reinforce the trust and credibility that is given to me to lead my ministry and steward it well.

There are a variety of methods for reporting your data. The data you are reporting and your audience will dictate the methods. Sometimes, a timely quote of a testimony is best to inspire, encourage and motivate stakeholders. For my staff, and myself we dive deep into the data to gain specific understanding of our ministry. However, when reporting to my supervisor and church leadership, I provide more of an ***Executive Summary***. Think of the executive summary like a dashboard in your vehicle. This allows you to take a quick look at critical data that will have great impact on your driving experience all while not having to take your eye off of the road for very long. The same is true for a Ministry Dashboard. This dashboard may not tell you exactly what is wrong, but it will alert you to the fact that something is wrong and needs further investigation and may need to be addressed soon. You will need to understand what these measures are for you and your ministry.

Note that an **executive summary** should provide stakeholders with a clear, but brief review of the important data you have collected.
Kotler and Armstrong (2006)

Financial performance is an easy gauge to monitor. Every month, you probably receive a report of your ministry's revenue and expenses as compared to what has been budgeted. This data informs you as to the financial performance of your ministry. If we are not careful, it is easy to use this as our only gauge of measuring ministry effectiveness. Tracking and reporting Ministry Opportunities for a specific program helps us to maintain perspective and not solely focus on financial issues. I recommend comparing Ministry Opportunities from a particular program to that same program a year ago. For example, if Ministry Opportunities for a specific program has doubled from the previous year, I would dive deeper to better understand why. Was there more money being spent to support these efforts? Were there more human resource support (e.g., sport ministers, coaches). This would help me make decisions on which ministries to focus more effort and resources on and which to reduce. Regardless of the size of your church and / or ministry, all of our resources (facilities, budget, staff, etc.) are finite. This is all a matter of stewardship. We are seeking to maximize the frequency and significance of the Ministry Opportunities that our ministries can produce.

When reporting, I use charts and graphs to communicate quantitative data. Then, provide a few quotes that capture the qualitative data you have gathered. Use pie charts only to communicate in terms of percentages. In fact, the only data I communicate via pie charts is church affiliation (Our church, "Other" or "None") and to compare which ministries generate what percentage of our total ministry opportunities. Pie charts do not have the ability to reflect trends across a measure of time. They simply look at the data at one particular moment in time. But, it is nice to be able to communicate that "X% of participants go to our church, X% claim another church as they are home and X% claim no church affiliation." I would argue that you should know these percentages and be able to share them at any time. Senior Pastors and church leadership also have a great appreciation for this simple, yet powerful data.

Bar and line graphs do a great job of communicating data across a period of time. Bar graphs are good for data reported in terms of months. More than twelve bars on a graph can be overwhelming and difficult to follow. However, you can stack two bars side-by-side to compare data by year. For example, to report Ministry Opportunities in January 2016 to January 2015, I would put those side-by-side and have 2015 represented by one color and 2016 represented by another. This helps quickly compare data to data to that from a year ago. Line graphs are excellent to use when reporting information with more than twelve data points, i.e., weekly or daily data. Line graphs are best used for communicating in greater detail and also provide for a greater ability to recognize trends. Often, I will use a Stacked Line Graph to see last year's data underneath this year's data. I do not worry too much about whether a particular week is above or below last year's. Often, major events do not fall on the exact same week every year. The primary function of the line graph is to see overall trends.

The following is an example of a line graph reporting Ministry Opportunities on a weekly basis compared to the same a year ago. I have also added a pie chart to show what percent of the ministry opportunities come from which programs. Note that the numbers within the graph and pie chart are not necessarily important, it is for you to visualize tracking possibilities:

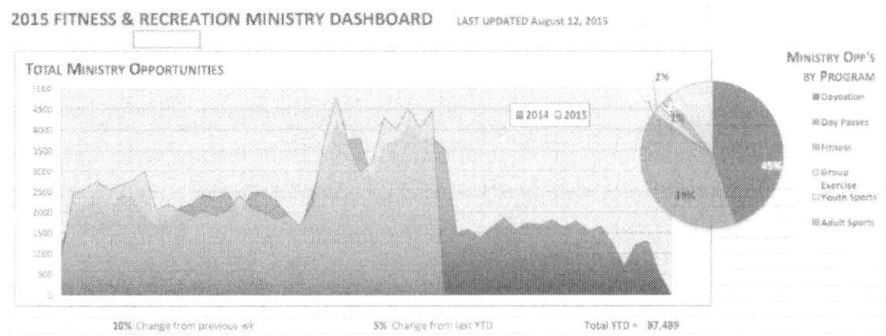

Below is an example of how I use a bar graph to report financial performance on a monthly basis as compared to a year ago:

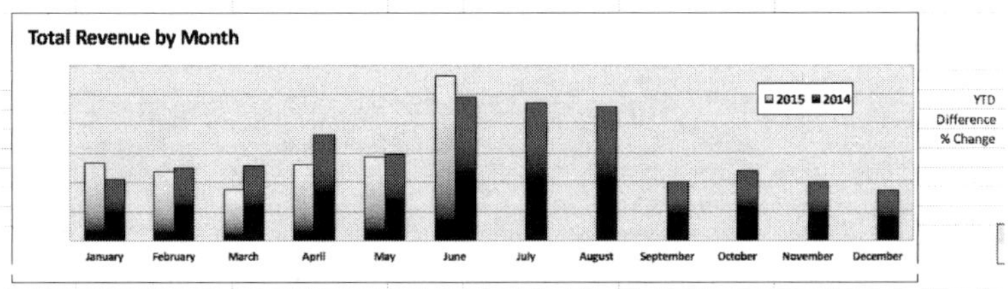

It is important to note that, up to this point, we have been discussing what I call Lagging Indicators. We are simply attempting to best track and report ministry that has already occurred. Leading Indicators are projected data such as forecasting budgets or anticipating ministry opportunities in a spring basketball league. There is an assumed amount of risk when forecasting. You are making an informed guess about future data, based on past data. The farther back you can look, the more accurate your leading indicators will be. For simplicity sake, if a program has grown by 20% every year for the past five years, it is fairly safe to assume that it will continue on that trend also knowing that past data and any anomalies that will skew the data.

Wrapping up

As with anything, there is a learning curve to tracking and reporting ministry effectiveness. My tracking and reporting methods today do not look the same as they did eighteen years ago. While constant tweaks and adjustments are inevitable, it is important to maintain some amount of consistency so that the data you are comparing year-over-year is the same. Using the example of reporting the Ministry Opportunities from the youth basketball league noted above, you would not want to change the game day multiplier from 3 to 5. This would greatly skew the data and falsely report growth when it may not be there in reality. Whenever you do need to make changes, it is important to note that to those you are reporting to. You could use an asterisk or annotation to bring attention to significant changes made. This helps maintain credibility in your reporting methods.

When gathered meticulously and reported effectively, both quantitative and qualitative data can be incredibly valuable to you and the ministry you lead. This helps stakeholders better understand the reality of your ministry, the value of it and its impact to the community. The ability to recognize trends helps with future planning by making informed decisions. Not always, but often, you are able to see where God may be at work and focus greater resources there. You are also able to recognize these victories and celebrate them with those that support your ministry and invest in it.

Learning-to-action exercise

If your local church does invest in sports ministry, ask the below questions. If your church does not, you may want to contact another church that has a sports ministry to work through the below exercise:

1. Why did your local church choose to invest in sports ministry?
a. What were the factors that led to starting a sports ministry at this church?

____

____

2. Make a list of all activities that are represented by your ministry.

____

____

3. Calculate the number of ministry opportunities each activity produces on a weekly basis.

____

____

4. Determine how data will be gathered and tracked. (Be sure to communicate why this is important to those that will be helping you.)

____

____

5. Update any registration forms to include any data you wish to track going forward, i.e., church affiliation.

____

____

6. Write down possible survey questions for program participants (and parents) to be conducted at the end of the next activity.

____

____

7. Create a spreadsheet used to track the data you are collecting. Below I have provided you with an example spreadsheet I use for tracking Ministry Opportunities. Working with this document, or a variation of it, on a frequent basis will build your confidence when using Ministry Opportunities to track the success of your sports ministry programs.

Additional Reading Resources

Chapter 1:

Bennis, W., & Goldsmith, J. (2013). *Learning to lead: A workbook on becoming a leader.* Basic Books.

Quatro, S. (2009). *Intentional outreach.* Xulon Press.

Robbins, S. P., DeCenzo, D. A., & Coulter, M. K. (2015). *Fundamentals of management: Essential concepts and applications.* Upper Saddle River, NJ: Pearson Prentice Hall.

Scott, D. (2014). *Contemporary leadership in sport organizations.* Human Kinetics.

Chapter 2:

Buechner, F. (1973). *Wishful thinking: A theological ABC.* New York: Harper and Row, 1973.

Buechner, F. (2013). The place God calls you to. Retrieved from http://frederick buechner.com/content/place-god-calls-you

Chart of National Congregation Study (2010). Retrieved from http://hirr.hartsem.edu/research/fastfacts/fast_facts.html#attend

Chelladurai, P. (2005). *Managing organizations for sport and physical activity: A systems perspective.* Holcomb Hathaway Publishers.

Keifert P. (1994). *The inviting and engaging Church* (VHS Video Series) St. Paul, MN: Seraphim Communications.

Lee, A. (2015). *Aspen Institute, 7 Charts that show the state of youth sports in the US and why it Matters.* Retrieved from http://www.aspeninstitute.org/about/blog/7-charts-that-show-the-state-of-youth-sports-in-the-us-and-why-it-matters

Meade, L. B. (1991). *The once and future church.* Washington, DC: Alban Institute.

Stoldt, G. C., Dittmore, S., & Branvold, S. (2012). *Sport public relations: Managing stakeholder communication. Human Kinetics.*

Thumma, S. & Bird, W. (2015, December 2). *Recent shifts in America's largest protestant churches: Megachurches 2015 summary report.* Retrieved from http://hirr.hartsem.edu/megachurch/megachurch-2015-summary-report.html

Chapter 3:

Council of Europe (2001). *Committee of ministers.* Retrieved from https://www.coe.int/t/dg4/epas/resources/texts/Rec(92)13rev_en.pdf

Harris, M., Chrisman, A., Sullivan, K., & Magehee, M. (1998). *The basics of life: Walking on the side of Faith.* New York, NY: Howard Books.

Chapter 4:

Adkins, T. (n. d.). *Developing your leadership pipeline.* Retrieved on March 17, 2016 from http://www.lifeway.com/leadership/free-e-booklet/

Charan, R., Drotter, S., & Noel, J. (2010). *The leadership pipeline: How to build the leadership powered company* (Vol. 391). John Wiley & Sons.

Maxwell, J. C. (2007). *The 21 irrefutable laws of leadership: Follow them and people will follow you.* Thomas Nelson Inc.

Northouse, P. G. (2015). *Leadership: Theory and practice.* Sage publications.

Rainer, T. (2013). *Thom Rainer interviews Todd Adkins about ministry grid.* Retrieved on March 17, 2016) http://www.ministrygrid.com/web/first-baptist-church-of-tampa/blog/-/blogs/thom-rainer-interviews-todd-adkins-about-ministry-grid

Robbins, S. P., Coulter, M. & Langton, N. (2006). *Management.* (8th ed.). Toronto: Pearson-Prentice Hall.

Smith, J. (Presented April 20, 2016). Understanding sports ministry from a management perspective. Presented at the 2016 REACHGathering Conference, Memphis, TN, April 19-21.

Chapter 5:

Jackson, S. E., Schwab, R. L., & Schuler, R. S. (1986). Toward an understanding of the burnout phenomenon. *Journal of Applied Psychology, 71*(4), 630-640.

Chapter 6:

Carson, D. A., & Keller, T. J. (2011). *Gospel-Centered Ministry.* Crossway.

Pew Research Center. (2015). U. S. public becomes less religious. Retrieved from http://www.pewforum.org/2015/11/03/u-s-public-becoming-less-religious/

Thumma, S., & Bird, W. (2011). *The other 80 percent: Turning your church's spectators into active participants* (Vol. 56). John Wiley & Sons.

Chapter 7:

Darlow, J. (2014). *Brands win championships: The secret to winning a national title in the 21st century.* Portland, OR: Jack and June Publishing.

Long Term Athlete Development (2017). Long term athlete development stages. Retrieved fromhttp://sportforlife.ca/qualitysport/stages/

McCown, L., & Gin, V. J. (2003). *Focus on Sport in Ministry*. 360° Sports.

Pitts, B. G., & Stotlar, D. K. (2013). *Fundamentals of sport marketing*. (3rd ed.). Morgantown, WV: Fitness Information Technology.

Chapter 8:

Bach, L. (1993). Sports without facilities: The use of urban spaces by informal sports. International Review for the Sociology of Sport. 28(2-3), 281-296.

Cole, N. (2005) Organic church: Growing faith where life happens. Josey-Bass Evenson, K. R., McGinn, A. P., (2004). Availability of school physical activity facilities to the public in four U.S. communities. American Journal of Health Promotion, 18(3), 243–250.

Kanters, M. A., Bocarro, J. N., Moore, R., Floyd, M. F., Carlton, T. A. (2014). Afterschool Shared Use of Public School Facilities for Physical Activity in North Carolina. Preventative Medicine, 69, 544-548.

Laughead, G. (2014, April). History of basketball: Dr. James Naismith, inventor of basketball. Retrieved from http://www.kansasheritage.org/people/nai smith.html

Lee, S. M., Burgeson, M. A., Fulton, J. E., Spain, C. G., (2007). Physical education and physical activity: results from the school health policies and programs study. Journal of School Health, 77, 435–463.

Luther, C. (2010, June). Coach John Wooden's lessons on shoes and socks. Retrieved fromhttp://newsroom.ucla.edu/stories/wooden-shoes-and-socks-84177

Martens, R. (1978) Joy and sadness in children's sports. Human Kinetics.

MyUpward Sports (2016). History. Retrieved from https://www.myupward.org/ Resources/Other/Careers/History/

Robbins, S. P., Coulter, M., & Langton, N. (2006). Management (8th ed.). Toronto: Pearson-Prentice Hall.

Stiles, J. M., Stiles, L. (2000). Mack and Leeann's guide to short-term missions. InterVarsity Press.

Steers, R. M., & Black, J. S. (1994). Organizational behavior (5th ed.). New York: HarperCollins College Publishers.

Spengler, J. O., Young, S. J., Linton, L. S., (2007). Schools as a community resource for physical activity: legal considerations for decision makers. American Journal of Health Promotion, 21, 390–396.

Warren, R. (1995). The purpose driven church. Zondervan.

p. 165 – Please remove all references from chapter 9 and replace with the following:

Pedersen, P. M., & Thibault, L. (Eds.). (2014). Contemporary sport management, 5E. Human Kinetics.

Thomas, Kenneth W. and Kilmann, Ralph H. Thomas-Kilmann conflict mode instrument: A profile and interpretive report. March 2010.

p. 165 – In Chapter 20 reference page place the following citation in alphabetical order with the other citations:

Scott, D. (2014). Contemporary leadership in sport organizations. Human Kinetics.

Chapter 9:

Pedersen, P. M., & Thibault, L. (Eds.). (2014). *Contemporary Sport Management*, 5E. Human Kinetics.

Thomas, Kenneth W. and Kilmann, Ralph H. *Thomas-Kilmann Conflict Mode Instrument: A Profile and Interpretive Report.* March 2010.

Chapter 10:

Kotler, P., & Armstrong, G. (2006). *Principles of Marketing* (11th ed.). Upper Saddle River, NJ: Prentice Hall.

Kouzes, J. M., & Posner, B. Z. (2007). *The leadership challenge* (4th ed.). San Francisco: Jossey-Bass.

About the Chapter Authors

Dave Bundrick
Executive Director of Upward Colorado
@davebundrick

Dave is a veteran local church sport and recreation minister. He has pioneered and led three different local church sport and recreation ministries. He earned a Bachelor of Arts degree in Recreation from the University of Mary Hardin-Baylor and a Master's degree in Parks and Recreation Administration from Texas A&M University. A licensed and ordained Southern Baptist Minister, Dave is an avid Mountain Biker and he and his wife are the proud parents of two school-aged children. Dave is widely respected as a leader in the local church sports outreach movement, has served on the CSRM Board of Trustees, including a term as Board President, and excels as an administrator with a forte in the area of assessing and evaluating the core competencies and success of ministries.

Greg English
Recreation Minister
Cool Spring Baptist Church
Mechanicsville, VA
@recreatn @coolspringrec

Greg is happily married to his wife Kelly and together they love to travel and cook. They have served in the sports and recreation ministry for over fifteen years both domestically and internationally. Greg and Kelly are the proud parents of son Tyler, and daughter-in-love Rachel, who live and serve in Lesotho, Africa. Brendan is the younger of the two sons and is an active volleyball player and works part time with his dad in sports and recreation ministry. Greg has been serving as the Recreation Minister at Cool Spring Church, VA since 2008. Greg is as an adjunct professor at Chowan University in the department of Sports Science and Physical Education teaching a Sports Ministry course. Greg currently serves as the Chairman of the Board of Trustees for the Association of Church Sports and Recreation Ministries.

Rich Green
Care & Support Pastor
Compass Christian Church
Colleyville, TX
@BoileRich

Born and raised in Indianapolis, Indiana Rich graduated with a Bachelor's degree in Sociology from Purdue University in 1981. He worked with the Fellowship of Christian Athletes (FCA) as the director of their National Conference Center from 1983-1992. Rich was hired on the staff at Mount Pleasant Christian Church in Greenwood Indiana as their first Sports and Recreation Director in 1996, after serving 4 years as the Sports Director at the Baxter YMCA. Ordained in 1998 he began work on a Masters In Practical Ministry from Cincinnati Christian University. For over 14 years Rich served as the Connections and Sports and Recreation Pastor, as well as the Point Person for Mount Pleasant being an "Intentionally" Externally Focused Church. He served two terms on the Board of Directors for CSRM, one term as CSRM's Board President and is currently CSRM Associate Staff for Special Projects. Rich has led numerous College Football and NFL Chapel Services and spent 2 years as Chaplain for the Indiana Pacers working alongside CBS Sports Analyst Clark Kellogg. He also served as the Character Coach for the Perry Meridian High School Football Program on the south side of Indianapolis. He moved to the Dallas, TX area in January of 2011 and spent two years as the Campus & Teaching Pastor for the Valley Ranch Campus of Compass Christian Church and is currently serving as the Care & Support Pastor for Compass at their Colleyville campus. In his new role with Compass he is excited about the opportunity to develop the Men's and Marriage ministries, as well as continuing the development of Sports & Rec Ministry as a part of Compass's community outreach emphasis. Rich served as the Conference Co-Host of the first ever REACHGathering in 2014, an international gathering of Church & Para-Church Sports Ministries held in the Charlotte NC area. Rich and his wife Patty (Married 35+ years) have 3 grown children a son-in-law and 2 daughter-in-laws, four grandchildren, and love being empty nesters!

Tinsley Jones
Director of Recreation Ministry
Crestwood Presbyterian Church
Richmond, VA

Tinsley has served as the Director of Recreation Ministry at Crestwood Church since 2011. She holds a Bachelor of Science in Kinesiology with a concentration in Sports Management from James Madison University. After working in Marketing for a packaging equipment company for several years, she returned to graduate school for a Master's of Arts in Christian Education from Union Presbyterian Seminary. After graduate school, Tinsley began her current position at Crestwood. Sports and recreation ministry has proved to be an exciting and rewarding challenge for her in discovering and employing meaningful, creative ways to blend sports and faith, as many do not naturally see the connection, which strongly exists. Although an avid sports fan in general, soccer remains her true passion. Tinsley coaches the youngest of players for a local soccer club in Richmond and still enjoys playing the beautiful game as well. Some life-long aspirations include remaining active, striving to learn new things, and owning her very own golf cart one day.

Chris Phillips
Lead Pastor
Journey Point Fellowship
Denver, CO
@chrisut

Chris served as the Minister of Recreation and Young Couples at Bellevue Baptist Church in Memphis, TN. He and his team have a heartbeat for connecting people to the local church to aid in their spiritual growth through discipleship. Before coming to Bellevue, Chris worked as a Medical Device Sales Representative for St. Jude Medical, Inc. He holds a Bachelor of Science in Sports Management from the University of Tennessee and a Master of Arts in Christian Ministry from Liberty University. Phillips is a CSRM Board Member and also serves on CSRM's Executive Committee. Chris is married to Libby, and they have the three sons and one daughter.

Jake Medcalf
Senior Pastor
First Presbyterian Church
Hayward, California
@PastorJakeM

Jake is the Lead Pastor for First Presbyterian Church of Hayward, California. Not only does he have lead pastor duties, but he also continues to work on sports ministry at his church. Jake partners with local churches to maintain the Crossover Basketball League for 3-12th graders. With a basketball gym on site, Jake and his team manages open gym basketball on Tuesday and Friday nights. Jake is also a participant on several sports ministry teams including the Basketball Fellowship League and a bowling League. Jake's previous sports ministry experience began in San Diego, California where he became the Founder and Director of the Diego Hills Basketball Academy where he raised and managed a budget of nearly $800,000. Jake also developed a summer sports camp for K-5th graders with an attendance of 150 kids.

Steve Quatro
Executive Director
Sports Outreach, Los Angeles

A husband, father, and grandfather (aka The Papa), Steve has been the Executive Director of Sports Outreach LA since 1992. Steve's efforts with this Outreach encourages and trains churches to employ sports to share the Good News of Jesus Christ. An adjunct professor, Steve was also a former CSRM board of trustee member and staff member. He is also the author of two books titled, *Intentional Outreach: A Guide to Simple Sports Ministry;* and *Church Planting and Sports.*

Bob Schindler
Director – Cede Partners
Huntersville, NC
@SportsOutreach

Bob is considered one of the leading voices for local church sports outreach and is one of the movement's most gifted communicators. Schindler has greatly shaped the theological and philosophical underpinnings for the Sports Outreach Movement and his analytical skills are appreciated by all who have worked to shape a truly Gospel Centered approach to ministry. Bob has served as the Executive Director of Church Sports Outreach (CSO), since 2003.

Prior to that, Bob was a church planter and senior pastor for 10 years and associate pastor for 8 years, all in East Tennessee. In both churches, Bob initiated sports ministries that served both adults and children, and were the primary outreach vehicle for both churches. Before entering the ministry as a vocation, Bob played professional golf for 4 years and was in both the chemical and software industries for six years. Bob studied Chemical Engineering at Vanderbilt University and is currently pursuing his Masters in Religion with an emphasis in Christian Thought at Gordon Conwell Seminary in Charlotte, North Carolina. Besides golf, basketball, and outdoor sports, Bob enjoys learning, analyzing and then synthesizing thoughts—especially about spirituality, sociology, psychology, and sports. Schindler was ordained in the Bible Church movement and is currently a part of the Evangelical Free Church of America (EFCA). His home church is Church at Charlotte, an EFCA church, where he and his wife are church supported missionaries. Bob is married to Beth, his wife of 38 years, and has four grown children, 1 girl and 3 boys, two daughters-in-law, and one grandson.

Jimmy Smith, Ph.D.
Assistant Professor
Sport and Physical Education
School of Education
Gonzaga University
@Sportsminwins
@JimmySmithPhD

Dr. Jimmy Smith is an Assistant Professor of sport management at Gonzaga University. Dr. Smith teaches sport management course in management principles, organizational behavior, marketing, fundraising and research methods. Dr. Smith earned a Ph.D. in physical education with an emphasis in sport management at the University of Alberta in Edmonton, Alberta, Canada. Dr. Smith's prior academic background experiences include a Bachelor's of Science degree in Kinesiology (Fitness Management) from the University of Nevada Las Vegas, where he also was a student-athlete with the baseball team. He completed a Master's degree from Central Michigan University in Sport Administration. During his time a Central Michigan University, Smith made his way up the ranks of the Central Michigan University athletic department working in areas of development and marketing where his primary duties included community outreach and revenue generation through sponsorship sales. Dr. Smith's current research agenda continues to focus on change and organizational behaviors in sport organizations especially with understanding sport ministry programs from a management perspective. Dr. Smith has recently published peer-reviewed manuscripts in the Journal of Sport Management, Journal of Issues in Intercollegiate Athletics, Journal of Contemporary Athletics and the International Journal of Sport Management.

Rev. Joe BW Smith
St. John's Lutheran Church
Lakewood, WA
@youravgpastor

Reverend Joe BW Smith is a redevelopment pastor at St. John's Lutheran Church (Evangelical Lutheran Church in America) in Lakewood, Washington. Pastor Smith has served congregations in Washington, South Dakota, Iowa, Wisconsin, and Denmark over an 18-year period. He has been involved in redeveloping congregations through pastoral ministry, interim ministry, mission planning, retreat facilitation, leadership training, team building, and consulting with congregations of several denominations, traditions, demographic profiles, and worship attendance sizes. St. John's Lutheran Church is a congregation whose primary constituencies are active duty and retired military households, and people climbing out of poverty. For a congregation that nearly closed for good in 2011, St.

John's is now connecting with its neighbors in a variety of ways; supporting youth basketball is one of those opportunities. Pastor Smith has a Bachelor's Degree in International Relations from Minnesota State University-Mankato, and a Master of Divinity from Luther Seminary in St. Paul, MN. His wife Melanie is also a pastor in the ELCA, and they have two daughters.

David Waddell
Lecturer of Sport and Recreation Administration
University of Mississippi, Oxford, MS

David is a long time veteran of recreation ministry and currently teaches Recreation Administration at the University of Mississippi. He has over 20 years of experience as a Church "Recreator" serving in four different recreation and sports ministry positions in Texas, Mississippi, Missouri, and Tennessee. David received his Bachelor of Science in Leisure Studies from Missouri State University and his Master of Religious Education with an emphasis in Church Recreation from Southwestern Baptist Theological Seminary. David is a respected leader within the field of recreation and has published two books. His first book is entitled: Holiday Biblical Characters: Finding My Stories in the Stories of Christmas and Easter. His most recent book entitled: Characters of the Bible: Finding My Stories in Their Stories. This book has received accolades from peers and is gaining popularity throughout an ever widening readership. In addition, Waddell has also written numerous articles for Lifeway Christian Resources. David is a sought after conference speaker known for his engaging, humorous and encouraging presentations. He has presented a variety of recreation workshop for CSRM Sports Outreach Summits, Rec Labs, and last year's REACHGathering. He is also a regular speaker for assorted regional and local conferences. Waddell is a CSRM Board member and serves on the Academic Partner team. David enjoys time spent with friends and family, including his ten grandchildren and entertaining all with his wit and unique perspectives of faith, life and what is important in life.